HOTSPOTS
RHODES & KOS

Written by Chris and Melanie Rice; updated by Jeroen van Marle

Published by Thomas Cook Publishing
A division of Thomas Cook Tour Operations Limited
Company registration no. 1450464 England
The Thomas Cook Business Park, Unit 9, Coningsby Road,
Peterborough PE3 8SB, United Kingdom
Email: sales@thomascook.com, Tel: + 44 (0)1733 416 477
www.thomascookpublishing.com

Produced by Cambridge Publishing Management Limited
Burr Elm Court, Main Street, Caldecote CB23 7NU

ISBN: 978-1-84157-892-7

First edition © 2006 Thomas Cook Publishing
This second edition © 2008
Text © Thomas Cook Publishing
Maps © Thomas Cook Publishing/PCGraphics (UK) Limited

Series Editor: Diane Ashmore
Production/DTP: Steven Collins

Printed and bound in Spain by GraphyCems

Front cover photography © Thomas Cook

CONTENTS

WHAT'S IN YOUR GUIDEBOOK?

Independent authors Impartial, up-to-date information from our travel experts who meticulously source local knowledge.

Experience Thomas Cook's 165 years in the travel industry and guidebook publishing enriches every word with expertise you can trust.

Travel know-how Contributions by thousands of staff around the globe, each one living and breathing travel.

Editors Travel-publishing professionals, pulling everything together to craft a perfect blend of words, pictures, maps and design.

You, the traveller We deliver a practical, no-nonsense approach to information, geared to how you really use it.

● *Stag Pillar at Mandraki Harbour, Rhodes*

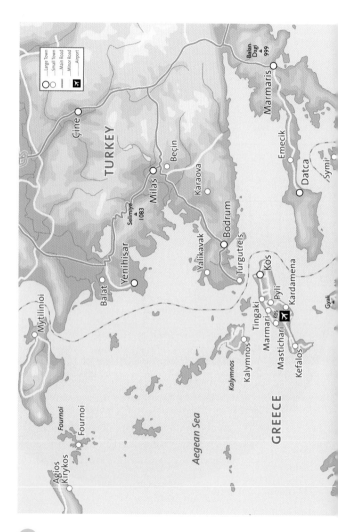

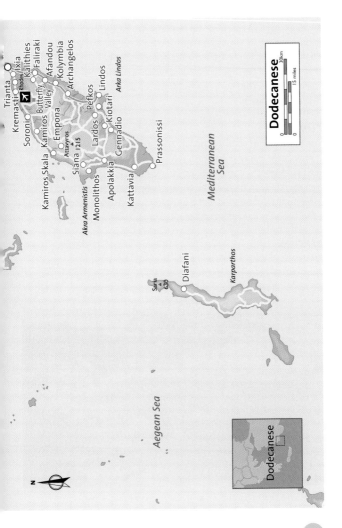

Dodecanese

Aegean Sea

Mediterranean Sea

Trianta
Kremastiti
Soroni
Ixia
Kalithies
Butterfly
Valley
Faliraki
Afandou
Kolymbia
Rhodes
Archangelos
Kamiros Skala
Kamiros
Empona
Pefkos
Lindos
Attavyros
Siana 1215
Lardos
Kiotari
Arka Lindos
Akra Armenistis
Monolithos
Apolakkia
Gennadio
Prassonissi
Kattavia

Satra
630
Diafani
Karparthos

Getting to know Rhodes & Kos

Rhodes and Kos form part of the Dodecanese, a group of Greek islands that lie just off the Turkish mainland, which is visible from many of the island beaches. The Greek capital, Athens, on the other hand, is a 14-hour ferry journey away.

CLIMATE

The weather is as good a reason as any for coming to Rhodes and Kos. If you're here in July and August, you can expect temperatures of 30°C (86°F) or higher and you're unlikely to see much in the way of rain (on average one day a month). The ancient Greeks put the wonderful climate down to the intervention of the sun god, Helios, and even today Rhodes holds the sunshine record for Greece (over 300 days a year).

BEACHES

The islands' beaches are some of the safest and cleanest in Europe. Over 40 beaches on Rhodes and Kos have a much-coveted Blue Flag for services and safety. You can drive to a secluded cove or inlet, take a boat

⬤ *The area averages just one day of rain per month in summer*

out to one of the islands, or simply soak up the sun on the nearest stretch of soft sand. The amenities, too, are second to none, with great opportunities for watersports – everything from calm pedalo rides to wild kitesurfing.

NATURAL BEAUTY

In the summer months, Rhodes and Kos are a riot of colour. The avenues of the tourist resorts are lined with palm trees, while extra shade is provided by broad-leafed fig trees, ancient planes, red-blossomed pomegranates, acacias, oaks and cypresses. Village gardens are ablaze with jasmine, honeysuckle, hibiscus and morning glory, while purple bougainvillaea trails from the whitewashed houses. The hillsides are planted with vines and, down in the valleys, you'll see orchards bearing a rich harvest of oranges, lemons, olives and figs.

CHURCHES

The walls and ceilings of Greek churches are covered with vividly painted, but rather sombre, images of Christ, the saints and scenes from the Bible. The main feature of every Orthodox church is the iconostasis, a wooden screen, gilded and filled with several tiers of sacred images, which separates the main body of the church from the sanctuary. Only ordained priests are allowed beyond this screen. If you want to hear a traditional Greek liturgy (the ceremonies have remained largely unchanged for centuries), mass is held in churches all over the islands during the week at 19.00. The main Sunday service usually starts at 10.00. Dress respectfully (cover bare shoulders and wear long trousers).

HISTORY EVERYWHERE

The story of these beautiful islands reaches back to Homer's *Iliad* and the Trojan Wars. There are reminders of ancient Greek civilisation everywhere – perhaps the most evocative are the ruined Acropolis at Lindos and the Asklepion in Kos. The Medieval Rhodes Old Town, complete with castle, has a magical atmosphere and is dotted with historic buildings – some of which have been turned into museums.

THE BEST OF RHODES & KOS

There's something for everyone on Rhodes and Kos, whether you want to laze on the beach, hike up the hills, visit monasteries and ruins, sample the local cuisine or take in the vibrant nightlife. To make it easier to choose, here's a list of the ten best things to do.

TOP 10 ATTRACTIONS

- **Admire** the spectacularly sited fortress of **Monolithos**, perched on a 235 m (770 ft) rock near the sea (see page 94).

- **Climb** to the **Acropolis at Lindos** on Rhodes (see page 49).

- **Explore** the underwater world by trying **diving**; beginners' dives are available at several resorts on Rhodes and Kos (see pages 61 and 108).

- **Hop on** an excursion boat for a trip along quiet coves, beautiful beaches and small islands; there are organised trips from most resorts (see pages 50, 61, 75, 78 and 106).

- **Sample** a different culture, try different foods and learn how to bargain on carpets or jewellery on a day trip to **Marmaris** or **Bodrum** in Turkey (see pages 82 and 85).

- **Take a boat** to the island of **Nisyros** near Kos (see page 89) and see steam rise from the crater of the volcano.

- **Take a day trip to Symi island** from Rhodes and wander the streets of the charming harbour town of **Yialos** (see page 96).

- **Visit the shrine** of the healing god **Asklepios** in Kos (see page 59).

- **Walk** around the moats of the spectacular fortifications around **Rhodes Town** (see page 16).

- Watch the sun set from a taverna in the mountain village of **Zia**, Kos (see page 66).

⬇ *Explore the Acropolis at Lindos*

SYMBOLS KEY

The following symbols are used throughout this book:

ⓐ address ☎ telephone ⓦ website address ⓔ email
🕔 opening times ❶ important

The following symbols are used on the maps:

𝒊	information office	○	city
✉	post office	○	large town
🛍	shopping	○	small town
✈	airport	■	poi (point of interest)
✚	hospital	—	main road
♥	police station	—	minor road
🚌	bus station		
✝	church		

❶ numbers denote featured cafés, restaurants & evening venues

RESTAURANT CATEGORIES
Restaurant price ratings (average main course plus starter/ dessert and drink):
£ under €12 ££ between €12 and €25 £££ over €25

▶ *Lindos, Rhodes island*

RESORTS
Rhodes & Kos

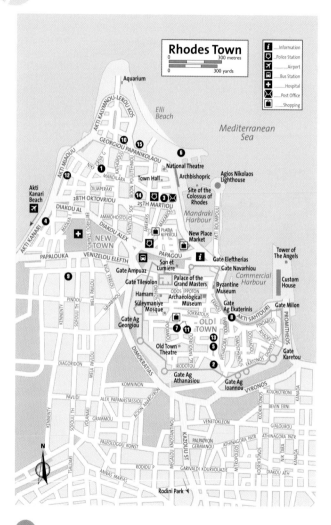

Rhodes Town

| 0 | 300 metres |
| 0 | 300 yards |

i .....Information
🚓 ...Police Station
✈ ....Airport
🚌 ....Bus Station
➕ ....Hospital
✉ ......Post Office
🛍 ....Shopping

Aquarium

Elli Beach

Mediterranean Sea

GEORGIOU PAPANIKOLAOU

National Theatre
Town Hall
Archbishopric
Agios Nikolaos Lighthouse
Site of the Colossus of Rhodes

Akti Kanari Beach
DIAKOU AL

28TH OKTOVRIOU
AMMOHOSTOU
DIAKOU ALEX
25TH MARTIOU

Mandraki Harbour

NEW TOWN
PLATIA KIPROU
PAPAGOU
New Place Market

VENIZELOU ELEFTH

Tower of The Angels

PAPALOUKA

Gate Eleftherias
Gate Navarhiou
Gate Ampuaz
Son et Lumiere

Commercial Harbour

Custom House

Gate Tilevolon
Gate Ag Georgiou
Hamam
Süleymaniye Mosque
Palace of the Grand Masters
ODOS IPPOTON
Archaeological Museum
Byzantine Museum

Gate Milon

Gate Ag Ekaterinis

OLD TOWN

SOKRATOUS

Old Town Theatre

IRODOTOU

Gate Ag Athanasiou

Gate Ag Ioannou

Gate Karetou

KOMNINON

DIAGORIDON

PAVLIDI
ALEX PAPANASTASSIOU
VENETOKLEON
KOLOKOTRONI
BEVIN ERNI

GRAMMOU
IOON ALIMEROON
PALPATRON GERMANOU
ATHINAGORA PATR
ATHINAGORA PATR
GIALOUROU

PALEOLOGOU KONST
KANADA

ANNAS MARIAS
RODIOU P
GARIVALDI KOURVOUAZIE
MITROPOLEOS
DIAKOU ATH

N

Rodini Park ◄

Rhodes Town

In its 2,400-year history, the 'City of the Rose' has seen them all: Greeks, Romans, Byzantines, Crusader Knights, Ottomans, Italians and, more recently, tourists. Rhodes Town, with a population of around 65,000, offers a range of historical sights as well as excellent shopping, a pulsating nightlife, some decent beaches and a good selection of places to eat. It's a great base for exploring the island too.

Rhodes Town presents a dual face – the Old and the New Town. The modern island capital, centred on Mandraki Harbour, is a cosmopolitan district of tree-lined boulevards, imposing public buildings, luxury hotels, international restaurants, intense nightlife and a dazzling array of shops. You will also find a casino and some beaches here.

The Old Town is the world's best example of a medieval walled town. The fascinating mix of cobbled streets, squares and courtyards, churches, mosques and massive fortifications is all dominated by the **Palace of the Grand Masters** and is surrounded by massive walls and a dry moat. The

● *Rhodes Town harbour overlooking the fortifications*

Old Town has two main areas: the Bourg (including the ancient Turkish quarter, bazaar and the old Jewish enclave) and the Knights' Quarter. Be sure to walk down Odós Ippotón (Street of the Knights), where the Orders' seven nations built their beautiful Gothic Inns or headquarters.

Rhodes was once the site of the ancient **Colossus of Rhodes** – one of the Seven Wonders of the Ancient World – a huge statue that dominated the city for 66 years before an earthquake toppled it. It probably stood on the site of the present castle, not straddling the harbour entrance as myth will have it.

BEACHES

Elli Beach (a few minutes' walk from Mandraki Harbour, on the tip of the Island) is the most popular beach in Rhodes. Sheltered from the wind, it has a diving platform as well as sunbeds, umbrellas and refreshment facilities, and it can get very busy in high season. The breezy Akti Kanari Beach to the west is quieter and more suitable for activities and watersports.

THINGS TO SEE & DO

Fortifications walk

The current fortifications were built between the 7th and 16th centuries and have survived sieges by the Arabs, Franks and Ottomans. The best way to get an idea of the scale of the inner and outer walls is to walk the newly opened routes through the dry moats. Entered from five points and provided with maps and information in English, you can walk part of the moat or go all around the Old Town. The lawns and trees in the moat offer good picnic spots, but there are no facilities so bring your own drinks and snacks.

Greek folk dances

The open-air Old Town Theatre hosts spectacular Greek dancing shows by performers clad in traditional dress. The theatre is signposted but is in a maze of alleys so make sure you can find it on time!

ⓐ 7 Andronikou ❶ 22410 20157 🕐 Every Mon, Wed & Fri at 21.20
❶ Admission charge

Hamam (Turkish baths)
One of only two Ottoman-era hamams that are functioning in Greece, this 15th-century bathhouse with its beautiful domes is great for a relaxing soak or a massage. Men and women bathe separately, and towels are provided.
ⓐ Platia Arionos 🕐 10.00–18.00 Mon–Fri, 08.00–17.00 Sat; closed Sun

Odós Ippotón Street (Street of the Knights)
Leading east from the Palace, this is said to be the oldest street in Greece. Following a 5th-century-BC layout, it is lined with fine medieval inns, which once housed the Knights of St John. The Inn of France is the largest and most impressive, with its magnificent crocodile gargoyles. The Inn of England is on Mousiou Square, and was abandoned in 1534 when Henry VIII was excommunicated by the Pope.

Palace of the Grand Masters
This formidable citadel was constructed by the Knights of St John in the 14th century and restored for Mussolini, the Italian dictator, as a summer residence. On the top floor you can view grand rooms with Roman mosaics of dolphins, seahorses, tigers, gladiators and mythical beasts. Downstairs, there's an excellent historical museum about ancient Rhodes, with displays on housing, temples, city planning, drainage, burial customs and the Colossus statue (see page 16).

RHODOS SIGHTSEEING
A reduced-price combined ticket can be purchased that allows entrance into four of the main sights of the Old Town: the Palace of the Grand Masters, the Museum of Decorative Arts, the Church of our Lady of the Castle and the Archaeological Museum.

ⓐ Ippiton St ⏱ 08.00–19.30 Tues–Sun, 12.30–19.00 Mon ❶ Admission charge

Sokratous Street

Colourful Sokratous Street is the street bazaar of the Old Town. Here you can buy everything from leather bags and jewellery to CDs and cuddly toys. At no 76 is a typical *kafeneion* (café) dating back to Ottoman times. The faded red building at the top of Sokratous is the Süleymaniye Mosque, founded in the 16th century to commemorate the Turkish conquest of Rhodes.

Son et Lumière (Sound & Light Show)

A dramatic re-creation of the siege of Rhodes by the Turks in 1522, culminating in the last-ditch stand taken by the Knights against Süleyman the Magnificent (not suitable for very young children).
ⓐ Pimini square, municipal gardens ☎ 22410 21922 ⏱ English-language narration nightly from Mon–Fri ❶ Admission charge

SHOPPING

The main shopping streets are around Platia Kipriou in the New Town, where you'll find Marks & Spencer and numerous boutiques. For traditional products you're better off in the Old Town where the shops along Sokratous street are a good place to start when looking for gifts such as wine, carved olive wood, natural products and icons. The Ministry of Culture museum shop near Platia Mousiou has reproductions of ancient artefacts, such as statues and vases. There's also a lively fruit and vegetable market on Zefiros Street every Wednesday and Saturday and on Vironas Street (near the stadium) every Thursday. The Nea Agora ('New Market') beside Mandraki Harbour has a handful of daily stalls selling fruit and vegetables.

TAKING A BREAK

Kringlan £ ❶ Nobody makes bread like the Swedes and this bakery café is the best place to sample great sandwiches, pastries and snacks.
ⓐ 14 I. Dragoumi ❶ 24410 39090 ❶ 07.30–24.00

Minos £–££ ❷ The roof garden of this pension at the highest point of Rhodes offers amazing views over the Old Town roofs. A great place for sunset and a snack. ⓐ 5 Omirou ❶ 22410 31813 ❶ 08.30–23.00

🔺 *Odós Ippotón is allegedly the oldest street in Greece*

Blue Lagoon ££ ❸   A restaurant, bar and pirate-themed adventure playland all in one. Inside is a ship, a lake, a haunted house and waiters dressed as pirates. It's great for children in the daytime, and wild by night too. In the same complex the Studio Gas plays dance music till dawn. ⓐ 2, 25. Martiou ⓣ 22410 32632 ⓦ www.lepalais.gr ⓛ 09.00–04.00

Capricci ££ ❹   This restaurant provides a high standard of cuisine and service, with a pleasant decor. Try their freshly cooked Italian food, with a choice of 16 different home-made pizzas, and enjoy stunning sea views at sunset. ⓐ 17 Akti Kanari ⓣ 22410 33395 ⓛ 19.30–late

Mandala ££ ❺   Healthy al fresco eating in the Old Town. By day a café serving coffee and cake, the Swedish-run restaurant turns out excellent Mediterranean food at reasonable prices in the evening. ⓐ 38 Sofokleos ⓣ 22410 38119 ⓛ 12.00–23.00

Meltemi ££ ❻   Named after the northern summer wind, Meltemi is the only restaurant on Ella beach and you can enjoy Greek home cooking and *meze* snacks while enjoying the view. ⓐ 8 Kountouri Square ⓣ 22410 30480 ⓛ 09.00–23.00

Romeo ££ ❼   Good-value, authentic Greek cuisine in an ancient setting at the heart of the Old Town, with live bouzouki music every evening. ⓐ 7–9 Menekleous, Old Town ⓣ 22410 25186 ⓛ 10.00–24.00

Alexis 4 Seasons £££ ❽   Upmarket eating in the gardens of the historical Naval Court judge's house, beside the city walls. Fresh fish and grilled meats in abundance, accompanied by fine local wines. ⓐ 33 Aristotelous ⓣ 22410 70522 ⓦ www.alexis-restaurant.com

Ammoyiali £££ ❾   Set on a hilltop, this stylish 'dream lounge' restaurant is worth a visit for its quiet setting and its international menu with fresh fish, steak and salads. After dark it transforms into a great cocktail bar. ⓐ 17 V. Iprou ⓣ 22410 23980 ⓛ 13.00–16.00 & 19.00–01.00

Ellinikon £££ ❿ Romantic atmosphere, outdoor garden and excellent Greek cuisine, just across from Casino Rodos. ⓐ 6 Papanikolaou ❶ 22410 28111 🕐 19.00–01.00

Fotis £££ ⓫ A seafood taverna with excellent cuisine, great service and a delightful atmosphere. A favourite choice of the local residents – always a good sign. Indoor and outdoor seating is available. ⓐ 8 Menekleous, Old Town ❶ 22410 27359 🆆 www.fotisgroup.com 🕐 08.30–01.00

AFTER DARK

Rhodes Town comes to life at night. Dozens of bars in the Old Town heave with revellers throughout the night, while larger, more sophisticated and louder options can mainly be found in the New Town. Orfanidou is the official 'Bar Street', appearing to have a disco/bar for every holidaying nation, but Diakou doesn't lag far behind.

Colorado ⓬ One of Bar Street's liveliest venues, which includes a live rock club and two discos. ⓐ 57 Orfanidou ❶ 22410 75120 🕐 20.00–06.00

Hamam £ ⓭ A former Turkish bathhouse has been converted into this charming bar with old vaulted ceilings, a pleasant terrace and a pianist playing on Fridays and Saturdays. ⓐ 26 Eshilou ❶ 22410 33242 🕐 18.00–03.00

Boudoir £££ ⓮ The snazziest cocktail bar in town with snacks and small menu. DJs nightly. ⓐ 26, 25. Martiou ❶ 22410 70971 🕐 08.00–02.00

Casino Rodos £££ ⓯ A glamorous casino with a restaurant and changing shows. The minimum age to enter the gaming area is 23; bring your passport and dress up for the occasion. ⓐ 4 Papanikolaou ❶ 22410 97500 🆆 www.casinorodos.gr 🕐 24 hours ❶ Admission charge

Ixia

Just a five-minute drive or bus ride from the amenities of Rhodes Town, Ixia (pronounced 'Ix-ear') is one of the most fashionable beach resorts on the island. Take a gentle stroll along the main street, Ialyssos Avenue (pronounced 'ee-ala-sos'), and you'll quickly become familiar with all that's available here, from the star-rated facilities of the luxury hotels to the neon-lit bars and restaurants catering to all ages and tastes. The long stretch of beach is never more than 50 m (55 yds) away, the sea is turquoise and translucent and there are views across to the mountains of Turkey.

◉ *Monte Smith – site of the Akropolis of ancient Rhodes*

Onshore breezes make Ixia absolutely ideal for windsurfing. Surfboards and pedaloes can be hired from stalls in front of the Rodos Hilton and Olympic Palace hotels. Swimming in the choppy seas is exhilarating for adults but young children may prefer the hotel pool. There's plenty of elbow room at Ixia, but if you want more privacy try one of the coves near **Psaropoula** (between Monte Smith and Rhodes Town). There is also a kilometre-long (½ mile) walkway along the coves near **Psaraoula**. It's great for an evening stroll, looking at the beautiful rock formations.

For a romantic evening walk it's difficult to beat **Monte Smith**, between Ixia and Rhodes Town, with its unsurpassed views over Ixia and across to the Turkish mainland. Monte Smith is named after Sir Sydney Smith, the British Admiral who observed the manoeuvres of Napoleon's Egyptian fleet from here in 1802, and it's only a short walk from the ancient acropolis of Rhodes.

THINGS TO SEE & DO

Coastal walk
Take a walk along a footpath which runs from Isia bay into Rhodes Town for a bit of exercise and great views.

Minigolf
Try your hand at the 18-hole minigolf in the cool, shaded gardens in front of the Olympic Palace Hotel. ⓐ Ialyssos Avenue ⓣ 22410 39790 ⓦ www.minigolf.gr ⓛ 10.00–23.00

> **SHOPPING**
> All the shops are on the main street, Iraklidon/Ialyssos Avenue. As well as a supermarket (**Pariners**) and bakery, you will find the jewellers **Gold Effie** and **Antoniadi Gold Bazaar**, the leather shop **Emmanuel Zannis**, and **Periklis** which sells hand-painted plates, jugs and other hand-crafted souvenirs.

Windsurfing

Windsurfers' World offers everything from lessons for absolute beginners to rentals for experienced speed devils. They also offer a jet-ski rental service.

ⓐ Ixia beach, in front of the Olympic Palace Hotel ⓣ 22410 24995 ⓦ www.windsurfersworld.gr ⓛ 09.00–18.00

TAKING A BREAK

Phillip's Bar £ Many devotees return year after year to enjoy Phillip's hospitality. Overlooking the rooftops of Ixia, the roof-garden serves full English breakfasts, sausages and mash, and mugs of coffee by day, English beers and cocktails by night. ⓐ 18 Venizelou ⓣ 22410 90366 ⓛ 08.30–02.00

Stani £ Excellent homemade ice cream; a great place to take children for wonderful ice cream creations served in large decorative dessert dishes. The beachside café has a swimming pool, sunbeds and a playground for guests, too. ⓐ Main road, in the Rodosland shopping mall ⓣ 22410 96422 ⓛ 09.00–02.00

Blue Palm ££ By day a pleasant, modern restaurant, by night a popular music bar with a selection of ice cold beers, daily DJ sessions and regular live bands. ⓐ Main road, opposite the Rodosland mall ⓣ No phone ⓛ 10.00–02.00

Fatman Slims Pub ££ Enjoy beer, sports and food from home at 'your local British bar'. Sunday lunch is a good time to come. ⓐ Main road, opposite Avra Beach Hotel ⓣ 22410 95492 ⓛ 09.00–03.00

Golden Wheat ££ Enjoy succulent Chinese dishes in this pleasant air-conditioned restaurant. Set meals for two and six. ⓐ 143 Ialyssos Avenue ⓣ 22410 96159 ⓛ 18.00–24.00

My Place ££ One of the first drinking holes along the coast here, this very homely Greek-run bar is decorated with team scarves from across Europe and serves good pub food and beers from across the world. ⓐ 42 Venizelou St ⓣ 22410 90794 ⓛ 09.00–03.00

Napoli ££ A friendly restaurant serving a wide range of pastas and pizzas, plus tasty traditional Greek dishes. ⓐ Ialyssos Avenue (near Hippocampus) ⓣ 22410 90119 ⓛ 12.00–24.00

Poseidonia ££ Smart Greek restaurant with garden terrace. Also has karaoke nights. ⓐ 9 Iraklidon ⓣ 22410 22276 ⓛ 09.00–22.30

● *The beautiful beach resort of Ixia*

Trianta

The name Trianta (sometimes spelt 'Trianda') comes from the Greek word for '30' and refers to the 30 stone houses that were built here by the Knights of St John in the Middle Ages. The resort is also popularly known as Ialyssos, after the sandy beach that runs along the coast here. This traditional Greek village on the Filerimos road rubs along nicely with its modern counterpart, only 500 m (550 yds) from the beach. Here you'll find all the usual tourist amenities from supermarkets and souvenir shops to family-friendly restaurants, bars and even a nightclub. There are regular buses to Ixia and Rhodes Town, while taxis are cheap and plentiful.

BEACHES

The pebble-and-sand beach at Trianta is suitable for swimming, but the water can be choppy and there's a strong current – young children should stay within the roped-off areas or swim in the hotel pools. Pedaloes and windsurfing equipment can be hired at the beach. There are more comprehensive watersports facilities at nearby Ixia (page 24).

THINGS TO SEE & DO

Children's activities
Luna Park miniature go-kart circuit Suitable for accompanied children up to the age of about ten. Buggies and motor bikes (including three- and four-wheeled bikes) all with seat belts.
ⓐ In Trianta ⏰ 10.00–22.00

Planet Z An indoor playground and café suitable for younger children. It is air-conditioned and safe, as the play area is enclosed and has floor padding and safety nets. Toys are also sold.
ⓐ Ialyssos Beach Road ☎ 22410 94874 ⏰ 19.00–21.30

Cycle hire

Mountain bikes are available for hire by the day and can be used for doing the shopping, getting you to and from the beach, or exploring nearby villages and resorts (Ixia and Kremasti for example). Energetic cyclists might consider making the trip to Filerimos on two wheels (5 km/3 miles, but a tough climb). **Ideal MTB Rental** ⓐ 3 Iraklidon, Trianta ⓣ 22410 93951 ⓛ 08.30–20.30

Filerimos

Just a short, picturesque drive from Trianta is the restored hilltop monastery of **Filerimos**, built by the Knights of St John on the ruins of ancient Ialyssos in the 5th century AD. The remnants of a Greek temple, the cross-shaped baptistry of the first Christian basilica, and the tiny underground chapel of St George, with 15th-century wall paintings, can all be seen in front of the steps that lead to the monastery. Roman Catholic as well as Greek Orthodox Christians worshiped the icon of the Virgin of Filerimos, in the hexagonal Church of the Knights, though at separate altars. To the rear of the monastery are the impressive remains of the Byzantine garrison. Running at right angles to the monastery is a tree-lined avenue known as **Golgotha**. At the far end of the path is a 14.6 m (48 ft) high cross that visitors can climb for breathtaking views of the island – even more so at sunset. As a souvenir of your visit, try *sette erbe* ('seven herbs'), a green liqueur produced by the monks.
ⓣ 22410 92202 ⓛ 08.00–20.00 Sat–Mon, 08.00–15.00 Tues–Fri
❗ Admission charge

SHOPPING

The main shopping street is Ferinikis, near the main hotels and parallel to the beach. For leather goods, clothing and gifts, check out **Pazouros**, **Panos**, **Olympos Gold** and **The Wine Cellar**. **Artemis Handicrafts** has handmade local products. **Anna**'s supermarket stocks newspapers, alcohol and groceries. Have your snapshots printed at the **Fuji Film Photo Shop**.

Mike's Horse Riding

A tiny stables on the road to Filerimos offers lessons and short treks for riders of all ages and standards.

ⓐ On the road to Filerimos ⓣ 22410 94277 ⓛ 10.00–13.30 & 15.30–19.30

Tourist train

Daily, 45-minute tours of Ialyssos by tourist train.

ⓐ Departs from the beachfront hotels ⓛ Between 10.00–23.30

Windsurfing

The bay is ideal for windsurfing. **Pro Center** stocks equipment, repairs sails and offers lessons.

ⓐ Beach ⓣ 22410 95819 ⓦ www.pro-center-rhodes.com ⓛ 09.00–18.00

TAKING A BREAK

Café Hellas £ This smart, typically Greek café (part of the Forum Hotel), with a shady terrace, is a good spot for afternoon tea. ⓐ Ferinikis Street ⓣ 22410 94321 ⓛ 09.00–24.00

Windmill £ This 500-year-old stone windmill has been converted into a convivial café and snackbar, and has a large terrace overlooking the picturesque beach. ⓐ Akti Kanari ⓣ 22410 94195 ⓛ 09.00–01.00

Bora Kai ££ Polynesian dishes supplement the Chinese cuisine here, where the menu features exotic names, like sea-treasure curry, Mongolian beef and Fiji duck. ⓐ Ferinikis Street, opposite the Blue Horizon Hotel ⓣ 22410 94328 ⓛ 18.00–24.00

Knights of Olde ££ Perhaps the best family restaurant on all Rodos – not just for the fantastic Greek food and the pleasant garden setting, but for the fast service-with-a-smile. ⓐ Ierou Lohou ⓣ 22410 94856 ⓛ 10.00–24.00

La Bonita ££ European and Greek dishes are served at this popular large restaurant opposite the windmill. There's a huge selection of fresh seafood, including lobsters, prawns and fish. ⓐ Akti Kanari ⓣ 22410 92001 ⓛ 10.00–01.00

Vrachos £££ Delicious upmarket Greek and international dining in an elegant beachfront restaurant. For something else than your usual steak, try the specialities such as ostrich fillet or boar. ⓐ 1 Akti Kanari ⓣ 22410 92220 ⓛ 11.00–02.00

AFTER DARK

BO Club A club on the main road, popular with the young set, and playing a wide mixture of music including hits from the 1970s and 1980s, house, disco and underground. ⓐ 2 Iraklidon ⓛ Bar open 21.00–24.00 ⓛ Disco open 23.30–05.00 ❶ Free entrance until 00.30

Cavo Tango ££ This café modelled after the white cube houses and blue-domed churches of Santorini makes for a great evening out as it's one of the better bars in town. Prices are a bit higher than elsewhere, but the atmosphere is unique. ⓐ 3 Ferenikis ⓣ 22410 90993 ⓛ 17.00–01.00

Kremasti

In small, friendly Kremasti, holidaymakers mingle happily with locals in the shops and cafés on the main village street. A world away from the commercialisation of the larger resorts, Kremasti is handy for exploring the picturesque mountain villages of the interior, yet just a short bus ride from the sights and nightclubs of Rhodes Town. Planes landing at the nearby airport frequently come closely overhead.

A stroll through Kremasti village reveals many hidden surprises. Most visitors will be familiar with the gleaming white tower of the **parish church** (a local landmark), but take a look inside. The walls are covered with delicately painted frescoes, showing scenes from the Bible and the lives of the saints, while the gilded frame of the iconostasis – the altar screen which is a feature of all Orthodox churches – is illuminated by flickering candlelight, creating an atmosphere of awe and reverence.

As you leave the church you'll see the men of the village congregating outside the local library. They come here to chat over a glass of coffee, to play backgammon or just to watch the world go by. Take any side turning from the main road and you'll come across traditional flat-roofed houses. Take a closer look at the courtyards where, under the lemon trees, families do their washing and cooking and even bed down under the stars on hot summer nights.

BEACHES

Kremasti beach, with views across to Turkey, is just several minutes' walk from the village centre. Loungers and parasols are available for hire and there are showers and café facilities.

THINGS TO SEE & DO

Butterfly Valley
A short drive inland will take you to **Petaloudes**, a scenic gorge which, from May to September, is home to the rare and eye-catching Jersey

tiger moths. These delicate creatures appear well camouflaged when their wings are folded, but are red in flight. There are shady walks through the woods and a restaurant with tables overlooking a waterfall and bubbling stream. If you're feeling energetic, a trail leads uphill to the 18th-century monastery of **Panagia Kalopetra** (❶ 22440 81801 ❶ 07.30–19.00 ❶ Admission charge), where there are wonderful views and picnic tables.

⬥ Kremasti parish church

Ostrich Farm

Visit the ostriches and other animals at this modestly sized farm. Try the ostrich burgers in the restaurant, or sample local dishes. Souvenir shop and playground for children on site.

🄰 On the road to Butterfly Valley 🄣 (mobile) 6945 327142 🄛 09.00–19.30 🄘 Admission fee, but free for children under 3 years

Strike Bowling Alley

Wind down in the evening with a game of bowling at the 8-lane bowling alley. Air-conditioned, serving cheap eats, coffees, cocktails and ice cream. Also has computers with internet access, a pool table and video games.

🄰 Eleftherias Avenue 🄣 22410 98344 🄦 www.strikebowlingclub.com 🄛 10.00–02.00

TAKING A BREAK

Grande Classico Café £ Café-lounge offering Greek cuisine for breakfast, lunch or dinner. Lively atmosphere and pleasant decor. 🄰 53 Eleftherias 🄣 22410 95595 🄛 08.00–04.00

Bee Garden ££ Chinese and Korean fare. Suitable for a special night out. 🄰 26 Kremasti Avenue 🄣 22410 94970 🄛 19.00–24.00

Café Verde ££ Set in a large, shady garden behind the Kahlua café. Great for coffee and cakes during the day, or cocktails at night. 🄰 Eleftherias Avenue 🄣 22410 98065 🄦 www.verdecafe.gr 🄛 10.00–02.00

Kahlua café ££ Kremasti's most popular open-air bar and café, overlooking the crossing opposite the church. The slightly kitsch decoration, complete with small waterfalls, makes for a pleasant setting for an evening out. 🄰 Eleftherias Avenue 🄣 22410 91498 🄛 10.00–03.00

The Village Inn ££ A lovely English pub under the airport flightpath serving everything from breakfast and snacks to tea. Use the terrace for the best views of the planes, and come on Fridays for the singalong night. ⓐ Niridon Street (the road to the beach) ⓣ 22410 95045 ⓛ 10.00–03.00

AFTER DARK

Babel A trendy bar and loung along the road towards Rhodes Town. There's ice cream, snacks, great cocktails and DJs spinning discs every night. ⓐ Eleftherias Avenue ⓣ 22410 90625 ⓛ 10.00–06.00

Melody Palace Smart club with live bouzoukia music and traditional dancing. ⓐ Eleftherias 69A ⓣ 22410 94920 ⓛ 23.00–05.00

Skybar A rocking café-bar on the corner near the classical library, with snacks and drinks served all day. Free wifi for guests. ⓐ 64 Eleftherias Avenue ⓣ 22410 91555 ⓛ 10.00–02.00

> ### SHOPPING
> Apart from the supermarket in Neriethon Road, most shops are on the High Street. **Foto Helios** has a 20-minute film-developing service. **Karelia** stocks English paperbacks and newspapers. **Scarpomania** sells leather bags, shoes, belts and canvas bags. The **Kremasti Fair**, renowned throughout the island, takes place between 8 and 15 August with craft and food stalls, music and dancing.

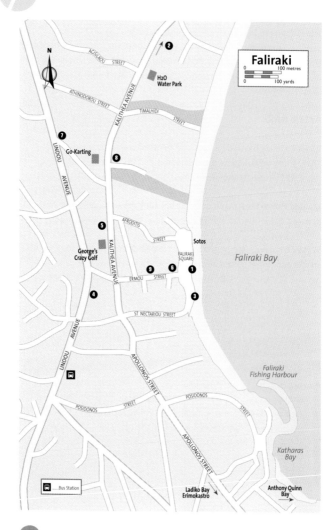

N

ACISLIOU STREET

ATHINODOROU STREET

H2O
Water Park

KALITHEA AVENUE

TIMALHIDI STREET

LINDOU AVENUE

Go-Karting

AFRODITIS STREET

KALITHEA AVENUE

George's
Crazy Golf

Sotos

FALIRAKI
SQUARE

Faliraki Bay

ERMOU STREET

ST NECTARIOU STREET

LINDOU AVENUE

APOLLONOS STREET

Bus Station

POSIDONOS STREET

POSIDONOS STREET

Faliraki
Fishing Harbour

APOLLONOS STREET

Katharas
Bay

Ladiko Bay
Erimokastro

Anthony Quinn
Bay

Faliraki

0   100 metres
0   100 yards

Faliraki

Faliraki (pronounced 'Faly-raki') prides itself on being the island's 'party resort' and the nightlife is certainly a major source of appeal. The beach is its other trump card – 5 km (3 miles) of golden sand offering every amenity for action seekers, including a full range of watersports.

There are lots of restaurants, bars and nightclubs in Faliraki, all within a 20-minute walk from the beach. **Ermou** is 'Bar Street' but the pavements of **Kalithea Avenue** also resound to the disco beat after sundown. Many bars remain open well after midnight.

Faliraki boasts one of the few genuine Scottish bars in the Aegean – at **The Tartan Arms** the waiters even wear kilts! There are karaoke bars, cocktail bars, sports bars and bars with giant TV screens showing movies or Sky sports. The clubs cater for all musical tastes – 1960s' nostalgia, garage, house and techno. Many are hosted by British DJs and there are theme evenings and laser shows.

Following several incidents of drunken loutish behaviour amongst partying tourists, the Greek authorities have come down hard on offenders. It is wise to be cautious when out on the town, and not do anything that might be deemed offensive or illegal.

BEACHES

All the beaches mentioned here have been given the coveted Blue Flag award. **Faliraki Bay** is gently shelving and is ideal for young children. Some 4 km (2¹/₂ miles) north is **Kalithea**, a thermal spa valued since ancient times. Nowadays, its delightful coves and beaches are much visited by scuba divers. For details of courses or information for certified divers, contact **Dive Med College** (ⓣ 22410 61115 ⓦ www.divemedcollege.com).

Katharas Bay (popular with nudists) has a sandy shoreline but steep rocky terrain to the rear. Scenic **Anthony Quinn Bay** (3 km/2 miles east of Faliraki) is a must-see, an inlet nestled between two mountains with rock formations jutting out into the sapphire waters. **Ladiko Bay** is a rocky cove with attractions such as the 'Seal's Cave' and the ancient fortress of **Erimokastro**.

THINGS TO SEE & DO

Boat trips
Hop on the *Marco Polo* for a daily 5-hour cruise stopping off at no fewer than seven beaches, board the *Sofia* for a shorter cruise held twice daily, or join Captain Tassos on the *Popeye* for one of several daily tours.
ⓐ Faliraki harbour

Go-karting
The small racetrack here is ideal for children.
ⓐ Between the Rhodes–Lindos road and Kalithea Avenue opposite the funfair ⓣ 22410 86151 ⓛ 14.00–23.00

Golf
George's Crazy Golf (ⓐ just off the main Rhodes–Lindos road
ⓣ 22410 85596 ⓛ 08.00–01.00)

H$_2$O
Relax by the pool or check out the disco. A snack bar is available during the day. Fri and Sat bazouki music and live entertainment.

ANTHONY QUINN
The Oscar-winning star of American movies Anthony Quinn shaped the popular image of Greece in no small degree when he played the title role in the film *Zorba the Greek* – remember Zorba's dance and the infectious music of Mikis Theodorakis? Quinn fell in love with Rhodes while filming *The Guns of Navarone* on the island in 1961 – several scenes were shot at what is now known as Anthony Quinn Bay, near Faliraki.

Ⓐ Kalithea Falirakiou Street ❶ 22410 87801 ❺ 24 hours; snack bar closes 23.00; disco opens 23.00

Tourist Train

All aboard the little train that shuttles between Faliraki Square and the hotels further along the coast. Also does excursions to various points of interest such as Kalithies village.

Ⓐ Faliraki Square ❶ 69377 00742

Water Park

Five different water slides, a wave pool, aqua gym, pirate ship and water guns. For the more adventurous, there are the Kamikaze and Free Fall rides. Food is available. Free bus from Mandraki harbour.

Ⓐ On Faliraki's coastal road ❶ 22410 84403 ❿ www.water-park.gr
❺ 09.30–18.00; until 19.00 June, July & Aug

Watersports and outdoor activities

Sotos (on Faliraki beach) offers water-skiing, paragliding, catamaran sailing (lessons available), snorkelling and pedalo hire (❶ 69422 34598 ❺ 10.00–19.00). Or take your life in your hands and go bungee jumping with **New World Bungee** (the crane is a local landmark). Just behind

● *Faliraki offers a full range of watersports*

the beach is the **Slingshot** – strap yourself in and enjoy being 'blasted into space' at a rate of 0 to 160 km/h (0 to 100 mph) in under three seconds. There's also 'sky surfing', combining the sensation of hang-gliding with the exhilaration of skydiving from a height of 45 m (150 ft).

TAKING A BREAK

Chaplins £ ❶ Lively beach bar, serving cocktails and snacks throughout the day. Theme nights and DJs. ⓐ Faliraki Square ⓣ 22410 85662 ⓦ www.chaplins.net ⓛ 09.00–03.00

Underground £ ❷ A family pub with pool tables, swings and karaoke, serving huge portions of English food including Sunday roasts. ⓐ Lido Road ⓣ 22410 86831 ⓛ 09.00–03.00

Dimitra ££ ❸ Greek taverna with over 500 menu items. Situated on the beach ⓐ Faliraki Square ⓣ 22410 85756 ⓛ 09.00–24.00

Golden Wok ££ ❹ Red lanterns and dragons decorate this eatery. Great for families as there is lots of elbow room! ⓐ Rhodes–Lindos Road ⓣ 22410 86143 ⓛ 17.00–24.00

Opera Restaurant ££ ❺ Beautiful atrium-style restaurant on three levels offering excellent international cuisine. ⓐ Kalithea Avenue ⓣ 22410 85776 ⓛ 18.00–24.00

SHOPPING
Musses (ⓐ Faliraki Shopping Centre) has a selection of dried nuts and fruits, sweets, coffees and chocolates, sold by weight. Visit **Obsession** (Kalitheas Ave.) for a fantastic selection of beach and party clothes.

Vinsanto ££ ❻ A shady café-restaurant with snacks, ice cream and cocktails, and good views over the square and beach. ⓐ Faliraki Square, above McDonald's ❶ 22410 86179 ❶ 12.00–02.00

AFTER DARK

The Castle ❼ Excellent nightclub in a castle, with a spectacular view of Faliraki. On three levels, pool bar with live bands, disco and jazz bar. More mature crowd than a typical Faliraki bar. ⓐ Rhodes–Lindos Avenue (just past the traffic lights, atop the hill on the right) ❶ 23.00–late

Maze ❽ This huge club holds over 3,500 people and is the main Rhodes venue for big-name DJs. Music suits all tastes and ages. ⓐ Off Kalithea Avenue ❶ 24.00–04.00

Venue Club ❾ Home of the legendary Hedkandi rave parties, this club is a favourite with young revellers from across Europe. ⓐ Ermou St ❶ 22.00–06.00

Afandou

Afandou (pronounced 'Ofan-doo') was deliberately built out of sight of the sea to protect it from marauding pirates (the name means 'invisible village'). That said, the main attraction of the resort today is the 7 km (4½ mile) long Blue Flag beach, one of the finest expanses of sand and pebbles on the island.

There is more to the 'invisible village' than meets the eye. Afandou's cultural heritage is on show in the beautifully decorated parish church and in a small museum in the grounds (🕓 10.00–12.00 ❶ Admission charge). One room features a typical kitchen sideboard with hand-painted ceramic plates, traditional wooden utensils and an old-fashioned loom with examples of hand-woven carpets; in the other room are displays of precious religious objects including vestments, silver chalices, bibles and painted icons.

While strolling through the village look out for old women wearing the hand-painted headscarves for which Afandou was once famous and take a peep into the courtyards of the houses behind Pernou Street. These are still used as second living rooms by many people (some villagers even sleep here on hot summer nights).

🔺 *Afandou beach is one of the finest stretches of sand on the island*

THINGS TO SEE & DO

Cycling

Cycling is a great way to get about and explore neighbouring resorts. Bikes can be hired from the **Motor Center**.

ⓐ 49 Pernou St (opposite Moka) ① 22410 51507 ① 08.30–13.00 & 17.00–23.00

Golf

Afandou's 18-hole championship course (par 73), designed by British golf architect David Harradine, is Rhodes' only course. Pros rate it as challenging but fair. It has a clubhouse with bar, changing rooms and equipment hire. The Rodos Open is held here in October.

① 22410 51451 Ⓦ www.afandougolfcourse.com ① 07.30–20.00 all year

Tourist train

Fun for the kids, the tourist train also saves grown-ups a 3 km (2 mile) walk to the beach. It departs from the centre of the village throughout the day, with additional stops at the Afandou Beach Hotel, the Lippia Hotel and the golf course. It continues around the village and resort (but not the beach) until 23.00.

SHOPPING

The main shopping street is Pernou where you'll find a pharmacy, several well-stocked supermarkets, souvenir shops, travel agents, a small CD outlet, sports outfitters and several restaurants. The **Kamara gallery** sells handmade pottery, model fishing boats and other Greek souvenirs. Gold and silver jewellery can be found at **Irinis Gold**. **Alko** (ⓐ 53 Pernou Street) has a good selection of local wines. **Gelateria Moka** (ⓐ also on Pernou Street) sells delicious Greek sweets and pastries like baklava as well as coffee.

Watersports

Mike's Watersports has jet-skis, wakeboarding, water-skiing, banana rides, crazy ringos and also speedboat tours.

ⓐ Afandou Beach ⓣ 69770 19950 ⓦ www.mikes-watersports.com
ⓛ 10.00–19.00

TAKING A BREAK

Golfer Restaurant ££ A shady terrace restaurant serving homemade specialities. Try the fried vegetables *à la maison*, moussaka or 'hole in one' – roast lamb rolled in filo pastry. ⓐ Rhodes–Lindos Road, opposite the entrance to the Golf Course ⓣ 22410 51861 ⓛ 11.00–23.00 Tues–Sun, 17.00–24.00 Mon

Life Garden ££ Set apart from the main Pernou Street, this family-orientated restaurant serves Italian, Greek and English fare. A helpful menu lists the ingredients of the traditional Greek dishes. ⓐ Pernou Street ⓣ 22410 52422 ⓛ 18.30–23.30

Lofos ££ A delightful bar set on a hill in the town centre – enter through the historical building on the small square and climb the steps for cocktails, cool breezes and great views. ⓐ Evripidou St ⓛ 17.00–03.00

Michalis ££ Informal Greek restaurant offering English breakfast as well as pork chops, mixed grills and kebabs. ⓐ 125 Pernou Street ⓣ 22410 51387 ⓛ 09.00–15.00 & 18.00–24.00

Reni ££ Serves delicious fresh fish and grilled meats. This is a great place, overlooking the sea, to watch the sunset over evening cocktails. ⓐ On the beach ⓣ 22410 51280 ⓛ 11.00–02.00

Sergio's ££ Watch the world go by from the romantic roof-garden while enjoying the mixture of Italian and Greek dishes. Air conditioning and satellite TV. ⓐ 3 Pernou Street ⓣ 22410 52050 ⓛ 18.00–24.00

AFTER DARK

Cream Club Party till the wee hours of the morning while enjoying luscious cocktails and great music. ⓐ Plateau Goumerobox ⏲ 23.00–late

Day and Night Listen to international and Greek music as you relax with an evening cocktail. ⓐ 36 Pernou Street ☎ 22410 52509 ⏲ 09.00–01.00

Life Bar A tiny bar run since 1986 by an affable Greek who loves 1970s–80s rock. There's a huge CD and video collection to choose from, and good drinks. ⓐ 39 Pernou Street ☎ 22410 53324 ⏲ 19.00–03.00

● *Afandou is a great place for watersports*

Kolymbia

Eucalyptus trees shade the main avenue of Kolymbia (pronounced
'Ko-lim-ba'), a smart, purpose-built resort overlooking Afandou bay.
The beach consists of a long stretch of fine golden sand ending at
Vagia Point, a small cove ringed by volcanic rock. Kolymbia itself has an
assortment of shops and restaurants and regular buses run throughout
the day to Afandou, Rhodes Town and Lindos.

Beyond Kolymbia the mountain road climbs to the local beauty spot,
Epta Piges ('seven springs'). Italian engineers built a reservoir here in
the 1930s – the waterfall in the centre of Kolymbia is part of the same
irrigation project. The original stream flowing from the springs has been
diverted through a dank and rather spooky 170 m (186 yds) long tunnel
to the man-made lake – if you're brave enough, you can wade ankle-deep
in the icy water. If you prefer to stay above ground, there is an alternative
route to the reservoir following a rugged footpath through the pine
forest. The scenic taverna attracts the crowds, especially at lunchtime.

A quieter spot is the little mountain village of **Arhipoli**, just 5 km
(3 miles) further up the road where you can relax over a glass of *souma*,
the potent local firewater.

⬤ *Kolymbia overlooks Afandou bay*

BEACHES

There are two main beaches – one by **To Nissaki restaurant** and the other by **Limanaki restaurant**. Both are gently shelving, perfect for swimming and safe for children. Sunbeds, umbrellas and pedaloes can be hired, but watersports enthusiasts and thrill seekers are better served in Afandou (5 km/3 miles) where you can hire pedaloes and water-ski, or try Faliraki (10 km/6 miles) where catamaran sailing and paragliding are available as well.

THINGS TO SEE & DO

Archangelos

The largest village on Rhodes, Archangelos is still relatively unspoilt by tourism and has retained many ancient customs and traditions. The people speak their own dialect, and their distinctive leather boots (which can be worn on either foot), have been adapted specially to give protection from snakes (you can buy a pair to take home if you can spare the time for a fitting). Alternatively, the local pottery workshops produce hand-painted plates decorated with traditional motifs. Archangelos is famous for its oranges, but you'll also see groves of lemons, figs, vines and olives growing beneath the ruins of the 15th-century castle.

ⓐ 5 km (3 miles) south of Kolymbia

Boat trips

Boats sail to Lindos every morning at 09.30, returning at 16.30. You can spend three hours in the town and the boat stops at two beaches on the way back.

ⓐ Kolymbia harbour ⓣ 22410 56250

Fun train

Join a 30-minute train tour of town departing regularly between 18.00 and 22.30. The train can also be used to get to Afandou beach with departures at 10.00 and 12.30.

ⓐ Kolymbia Square

Minigolf

Try the minigolf in the pretty garden of **Kolimpia Star**, a popular café.
ⓐ Near Hotel Tropical ❶ 22410 56309 🕐 10.00–01.00, or later

Tsampika

The hilltop monastery takes its name from the *tsampas* (sparks) which lit up the sky when an icon from a church on Cyprus miraculously materialised on Rhodes. (The Cypriots reclaimed the icon three times but it kept returning until they eventually let it be.) Every year on 8 September local women make a pilgrimage to Tsampika to pray for fertility. If their prayers are answered with a boy, he is called Tsampikos; if a girl, Tsampika. There are commanding views of the coast from the monastery, while the beach below is unspoilt and ideal for sun-worshippers.

TAKING A BREAK

Brillantina £ This café-bar with a cool, shady terrace, in the Brillante complex, also serves pizzas and delicious ice cream.
ⓐ Eucalyptus Avenue ❶ 22410 56369 🕐 11.00–24.00 or later

Carrusel £ A cheap and cheerful Greek restaurant. Try the chicken *souvlaki* and the *gyros*. ⓐ Eucalyptus Avenue ❶ 22410 56085
🕐 11.00–24.00

Limanaki ££ Come to this bright blue taverna and waterfalls for good food, beautiful views over the coastline and the best sunsets in Kolymbia. ⓐ Limanaki beach ⓣ 22410 56240 ⓛ 12.00–24.00; drinks from 09.00

Panoramic ££ Standing 300 m (985 ft) high above the resort, this rustic restaurant serves local dishes and home-made bread, while you experience the most magical views across the interior of Rhodes. ⓐ Tsampika monastery ⓣ (mobile) 62460 61262 ⓛ 09.00–20.00

Savvas ££ The speciality in this Greek restaurant is a mouthwatering and bargain-priced mixed grill (for two persons). ⓐ Eucalyptus Avenue ⓣ 22410 56300 ⓛ 11.00–22.00

To Nissaki ££ A simple bar and taverna right on the beach. Try the mixed fish platter washed down with Rhodian wine from the village of Empona. ⓐ Kolymbia beach ⓣ 22410 56360 ⓛ 11.00–24.00

AFTER DARK

Memories £ The large-screen TV is a popular feature here. ⓐ Eucalyptus Avenue ⓣ 22410 56502 ⓛ 16.00–01.00

Oasis £ A large café-bar near the beach with satellite TV, cocktails, crêpes and other snacks. Bands perform twice a week in high season. ⓐ Eucalyptus Street ⓣ 69344 60850 ⓛ 10.00–03.00

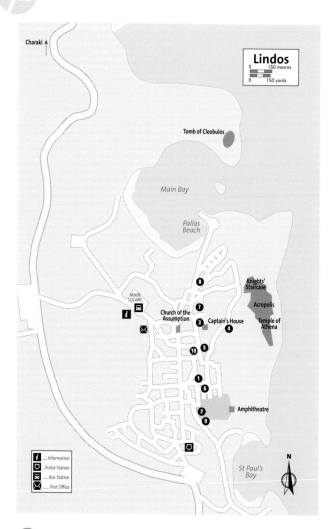

Charaki

Tomb of Cleobulos

Main Bay

Pallas Beach

Lindos
0   150 metres
0   150 yards

MAIN SQUARE

Knights' Staircase

Acropolis

Temple of Athena

Church of the Assumption

Captain's House

Amphitheatre

St Paul's Bay

N

i ......Information
......Police Station
......Bus Station
......Post Office

Lindos

St Paul visited Lindos in AD 58 and found a wealthy and prosperous community with a history stretching back at least 1,500 years. The Acropolis, with its ruined Temple of Athena, is the jewel in the crown of this Grade 1 archaeological site, where cars and bikes are outlawed and the only means of transport is by donkey. Visitors can enjoy a drink in one of the old seafarers' houses, admire the local pottery and needlework on display in the narrow cobbled streets and take a cooling dip in the bay.

All signs in Lindos point to the **Acropolis** (📞 22440 31258 🕐 08.00–19.00 Tues–Sun). Resist the temptation to buy 'traditional' embroidery along the way – most of it is imported and overpriced. At the foot of the **Knights' Staircase** (leading to the castle) is a large relief of a trireme (the ancient Greek sailing ship) which was carved out of the rock in the 2nd century BC.

The Knights built their stronghold on the foundations of the classical city, so today visitors can see the remains of both. Look out for the lofty chambers of the commander's palace, the remaining columns of an 87 m (95 yds) long portico and the regal flight of steps leading to the ruined 4th-century-AD **Temple of Athena** (patron goddess of Lindos). From here there are fabulous views over **Pallas beach** in one direction and the azure-blue waters of **St Paul's Bay** in the other. The most novel way of approaching the Acropolis is by donkey (the so-called 'Lindos taxi'). If you pay extra, you can have a photograph as a souvenir. The Acropolis is being renovated, and parts will be closed off until 2009.

BEACHES

Water-skiing, pedaloes and parascending are all available from the small **Pallas** beach in Main Bay, where there is also a roped-off safe area for children. Sunbeds and parasols are also available in **St Paul's Bay**.

● *St Paul's Bay is the perfect relaxation spot*

THINGS TO SEE & DO

Boat trips

Catch the once-weekly boat to Rhodes Town for some shopping.
Alternatively, climb aboard one of the daily excursion boats which
explore the south-eastern coast, with swimming stops.

Captain's House

Many local seafarers' houses, similar to this one, date from the 16th and
17th centuries, and have now been converted to restaurants and bars.
Look out for the tell-tale features: rope coils and other nautical motifs
on doorways, painted ceramic plates hanging from the interior walls
(kept as souvenirs of voyages) and balconied courtyards with distinctive
pebble mosaic floors known as *choklaki*. **Captain's House Bar**, now
a classical music bar, can be seen en route to the Acropolis.
ⓐ 243 Acropolis Street ⓣ 22440 31235 ⓛ 08.00–early morning

Church of the Assumption

The red-tiled domes and elegant bell tower of this delightful Byzantine church are a local landmark. In the 18th century the walls, ceilings – and even the pulpit – were covered with frescoes. The vivid *Last Judgement* on the back wall was a reminder to all of their mortality.
🕐 09.00–12.00 & 16.00–19.00

EXCURSIONS
Charaki

This attractive fishing village (pronounced 'Har-aki'), north of Lindos, is a developing resort. Overlooking the beach is the formidable castle of **Feraklos**, the last stronghold on the island to be captured by the Turks.

TAKING A BREAK

Bacco Restaurant £ ❶ Delicious international cuisine in the heart of Lindos. Roof garden and music. ⓐ Above Luna Bar ☏ 22440 31431
🕐 17.00–01.00

Swedeo £ ❷ Fantastic Swedish ice cream, bakery products, waffles and pastries, served in a small café near the ancient theatre. ⓐ Lindos village
☏ 22410 31233 🕐 09.00–23.00

● *View of Lindos across the main bay*

Aphrodite ££ ❸ Attractive fish restaurant with roof-garden, popular with local residents. International cuisine. ● Akropoleos Street ❶ 22440 31255 ● 18.00–23.30

Caesar's Restaurant ££ ❹ Halfway up to the Acropolis, this is a great place to stop for juice or a light snack in the day, or a romantic meal in the evening on the vine-clad patio or roof-terrace. Traditional Greek cuisine. ● Akropoleos Street ❶ 22440 31410 ● 08.00–01.00

Cyprus Taverna ££ ❺ Also known as Timi's Place, this restaurant serves Cypriot specialities, like *seftalies* (grilled mincemeat with spices), plus chicken and fish dishes. ⓐ 191 Akropoleos Street ❶ 22440 31539 🕐 11.00–15.00 & 18.00–23.00

Sinatras ££–£££ ❻ An old house has been converted into a restaurant with good international and Greek dishes, and of course plenty of pictures of Sinatra on the walls. ⓐ Lindos village ❶ 22440 31741 🕐 09.30–12.30 & 19.00–23.00, bar until 03.00

Village Café ££–£££ ❼ Excellent, healthy fresh salads, sandwiches, croissants, bagels, pies and ice cream creations served in a quiet cobbled courtyard. ⓐ Lindos village ❶ 22410 31559 🕐 09.00–24.00

Broccolino £££ ❽ A funky Italian restaurant decorated with mosaics of pottery and mirror shards. Sit in the courtyard beneath the vines for the delicious starters, pastas and meat dishes. ⓐ Lindos village ❶ 22440 31688 🕐 11.00–15.00 & 19.00–23.30, bar until 01.00

Pallazetto £££ ❾ A beautiful Italian-owned restaurant set around a courtyard for delectable pasta, meat and fish dishes, and pizzas cooked in wood ovens. ⓐ Near St Paul's Bay and Amphitheatre ❶ 22440 31612 🕐 18.00–24.00

AFTER DARK

Museum Bar ££ ❿ Plasma screens with live sports hang on the walls of this deliciously air-conditioned bar. Enjoy drinks, snacks or baguettes while you catch a match. ⓐ Lindos village ❶ 22440 31446 🕐 08.30–02.00

Pefkos, Lardos & Kiotari

The developing southern resorts of Pefkos, Lardos and Kiotari are best known for their leisurely pace of life and their often deserted beaches. Their low-key nightlife is centred around traditional tavernas and the friendly bars, although the more lively nightlife of Lindos is never far away. Set amidst pine trees in a picturesque bay just 5 km (3 miles) south of the busy resort of Lindos, Pefkos (meaning 'pine tree') was once the Lindians' summer hide-away. Now it is a popular, laid-back resort in its own right, with smart new holiday accommodation and a good selection of restaurants, shops and bars scattered along the main road and on the street leading to its long, sandy beach.

South of Pefkos, the popular international resort of Lardos is centred on a traditional Greek village, set in pretty countryside 2 km (1 mile) inland. With a wide variety of sand-and-pebble beaches, coves and rocky inlets to choose from on the stretch of coast between Pefkos and Lardos, an excellent range of watersports, and a go-karting track on the village outskirts, the village is quite sleepy during the day. By night, however, village life centres around an array of traditional tavernas, fish restaurants and bars in the main square.

⬛ *Pefkos is a popular get-away*

THINGS TO SEE & DO

Lardos Go-Karts

Speed around a 700 m (760 yd) track. There are regular karts as well as special ones for children.

ⓐ Lardos–Pefkos road ⓣ 22440 44510 ⓛ 09.30–23.00

Minigolf

Hellas mini Golf has a varied new course along the main road, lit up after dark so you can practise your swing all night.

ⓐ Lardos–Lindos road ⓣ 22440 44332 ⓛ 10.00–01.00

Prassonissi

Prassonissi or 'Leek Island' marks Rhodes' southernmost extremity, where the Aegean Sea meets the Mediterranean – a paradise for windsurfers. From May to September it is possible to stroll across the broad, sandy causeway that links Prassonissi to the rest of Rhodes, but during winter it is cut off by high seas.

Thari Monastery

The oldest surviving religious foundation on Rhodes has recently been re-established and the 9th-century monastery church is open to the public. Glorious frescoes of the Apostles and the prophets cover the apse and dome while, in the nave, unusual biblical scenes are depicted, such as the storm on the Sea of Galilee.

ⓛ 10.00–18.00

Watersports

The **Lardos Skiing and Fun Centre** at St George's Hotel (ⓐ Aghios Georgios) offers water-skiing and parasailing or go to Pefkos Waterfun (ⓣ 69324 33498) on the main beach, where you can rent pedaloes and canoes and speed boats.

TAKING A BREAK

Red Dragon £–££ Good Chinese food to eat in or take away. The set menus are good value. **ⓐ** Pefkos Square **ⓣ** 22440 48392 **ⓛ** 16.00–00.30

Coralli ££ Local cuisine, a pretty pool overlooking the beach, delicious cocktails and entertainment nights. **ⓐ** Pefkos–Lardos Road, Lardos **ⓣ** 22440 48425 **ⓛ** 09.00–01.00

Greek House ££ Try the range of fantastic crêpes, or sit in for delicious Greek cuisine of grilled meats or fish. **ⓐ** Pefkos beach road **ⓣ** 22440 48167 **ⓛ** 17.00–23.30

Kelari Bar ££ Relax to great music in this bar specialising in a range of cocktails, beers and spirits. **ⓐ** 100 m (109 yds) from Pefkos beach Road **ⓣ** 22440 48357 **ⓛ** 17.00–03.00

Loukas ££ Delicious charcoal-grilled meat dishes, steaks, fresh fish and salads in the lively town centre of Lardos. **ⓐ** Lardos Square **ⓣ** 22440 44304 **ⓛ** 10.00–23.00

Pane di Capo ££ A popular café-restaurant serving fresh bread, pastries and muffins, ice cream, waffles and filling breakfasts. **ⓐ** Pefkos main road **ⓣ** 22440 48302 **ⓛ** 08.00–02.00

Lee Beach ££–£££ Creative Mediterranean cuisine served on a breezy terrace with views over the main beach. At night, the upstairs bar opens. **ⓐ** Pefkos beach road **ⓣ** 22440 48213 **ⓛ** 09.30–24.00

AFTER DARK

Eclipse Bar A landscaped complex with bars, sunbeds, a pool and an amazing curtain waterfall. There are regular parties with DJs and large screen TVs. **ⓐ** Pefkos Square **ⓣ** 22440 48335 **ⓛ** 10.00–01.00

Kos Town

The capital of Kos island is an attractive and lively port, with shady tree-lined avenues and lush green spaces brightened by lilac, jasmine and hibiscus. Kos town's sights include two mosques, a medieval castle and ancient remains, most notably the Asklepion, perhaps Europe's oldest health resort. The beaches offer a variety of watersports, while boat excursions leave from the harbour for the neighbouring islands.

A miniature train (the **Dotto train**) takes visitors on a 15-minute whistle-stop tour of the town centre, departing from the harbour at half-hourly intervals from 10.00 to 14.00 and 18.00 to 20.00.

Guarding the port, and its clutter of yachts and motor vessels, is the **Castle of the Knights of St John**, built in the 14th and 15th centuries with a massive outer wall and keep which look impregnable even today (🕒 08.00–19.30 Tues–Sun ❶ Admission charge). Alongside is an avenue lined with palm trees; this was originally the moat, which separated the castle from the town.

Nearby, you will find **Hippocrates' plane tree**. It may not really have sheltered the ancient Greek physician, but it is at least 700 years old and boasts a trunk 17 m (19 yds) in circumference. Overlooking the tree is an 18th-century **Turkish mosque** and, nearby, the ruins of the agora, a market-cum-shopping arcade, dating back to the 4th century BC. Today's shoppers head for the fruit and vegetable market in Eleftherias Square and the pedestrianised '**Old Bazaar**' on Ifestou Street.

BEACHES

The **town beach**, east of the harbour, becomes crowded very early in the day. A better bet, also called **Town Beach**, is about 500 m (550 yds) west of the centre (bus no 2) where you can windsurf or paraglide. There are plenty of tavernas and snack bars nearby, and it is close to the discos and water facilities. For somewhere quieter and less congested, head for **Tingaki**, a little further west, or **Psalidi** on the other side of town (bus no 1).

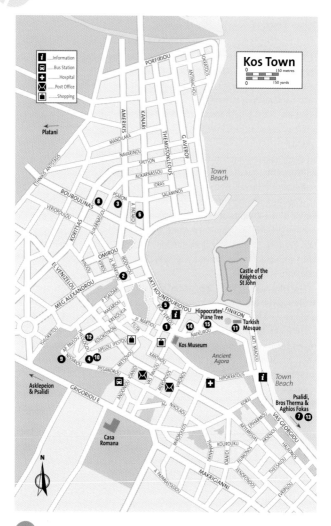

Both have watersports facilities. Beyond Psalidi, **Aghios Fokas** beach has volcanic black sand and is often deserted.

THINGS TO SEE & DO

Archaeological treasures

The town centre contains the ruins of the Roman agora (market), a running track, an amphitheatre and the **Casa Romana**, a restored Roman villa containing fine mosaics and murals (currently closed for repairs but due to re-open in 2008). Further treasures can be seen in **Kos Museum** (ⓐ Eleftherias Square ⓣ 22420 28326 ⓛ 08.00–15.30 Tues–Sun ⓘ Admission charge), including an ancient statue of Hippocrates and a beautiful mosaic of Hippocrates welcoming Asklepios to Kos.

Asklepion and Platani

Dedicated to Asklepios, the Greek god of healing, this ancient medical centre, which comprised hostels, baths, temples and recovery rooms, followed the teachings of Hippocrates, who was born on Kos in the 5th century BC; doctors still take the Hippocratic Oath today. There are superb views from the pine-clad hill high above the town. The tourist train leaves from near the tourist information office at half-hourly intervals (ⓛ 10.00–14.00 & 18.00–20.00, journey time 20 minutes). Platani is a charming village on the outskirts of Kos Town, halfway to Asklepion. A minority of Muslims of Turkish descent live here, and this is reflected in

HIPPOCRATES

According to legend, the famous Greek physician was born on Kos around 460 BC. The 'father of Western medicine' encouraged his followers to observe patients' symptoms, rather than attributing all illness to the wrath of the gods. The **Asklepion**, one of more than 200 shrines built, is among the most famous in the world, and is dedicated to the god of healing – Asklepios.

⬥ Visit ancient ruins in Kos Town

the dishes served at the restaurants around the small main square; you can ask to get off the tourist train for lunch on the way back.

🕒 08.00–19.30 Tues–Sun ❶ Admission charge

Boat trips

Kos harbour is crammed with boats doing scheduled trips to Rhodes, Nisyros, Symi, Patmos, and to Bodrum in Turkey (for which you need to book in advance and bring your passport). The most popular excursion however is the three-island tour to Krevatia, Kalymnos and Pserimos, which stops off at various bays and beaches. Stroll past the waterfront in the evening to see what's on offer and to book your tickets for the next day.

Diving

Kos Divers offers everything from PADI courses for beginners to expert deep and night dives.

ⓐ Hotel Kipriotis Village, Psalidi ❶ 22420 21553 Ⓦ www.kosdivers.com

Go-kart racing

There is a track just west of the town at Psalidi.

ⓐ Main road, Psalidi ❶ 22420 25897 🕒 09.00–23.00

Platani

A charming village 3 km (2 miles) west of Kos Town, where Greek Orthodox people live peacefully together with Muslims of Turkish descent. It is also a popular lunch stop on the way back from the Asklepion.

Psalidi

Psalidi is really just an extension of Kos Town, a peaceful overflow of hotels, bars and waterfront restaurants. Its real attraction, however, is the hot spring of **Bros Therma**, which runs directly into the sea 5 km (3 miles) beyond **Aghios Fokas** beach, where you can bathe away your aches and pains in the warm sulphuric spring water in a man-made rock pool at the water's edge.

TAKING A BREAK

Chocolat Bakery £ ❶ Pastries, pies, sandwiches, ice cream and other sweet snacks served with a smile. Find Chocolat near the museum.
ⓐ A. Ioannidi ⓛ 08.00–23.00

Del Mare £ ❷ Not just a pleasant café and bar attracting a young local crowd, there's an Internet café in the back room where you can keep in touch with the family back home. ⓐ 4 Meg. Alexandrou Street
ⓣ 22420 24244 ⓦ www.cybercafe.gr ⓛ 09.00–01.00 ⓘ No food

Hellas £–££ ❸ A highly recommended family taverna with simple but delicious Greek and international dishes. Ask to try one of many local specialities. ⓐ 7 Psaron Street ⓣ 22420 22609 ⓛ 10.00–23.00

Elia ££ ❹ This hundred-year-old building filled with antiques is now home to a great traditional Greek restaurant. Try the selection of meze snacks, including cheeses, pies, meat and fresh fish. ⓐ 27 Apelou Ifestou
ⓣ 22420 22133 ⓦ www.elia-kos.gr ⓛ 09.00–23.00

Fish House ££ ❺ A touristy but fun seafood restaurant at the top of some picturesque stairs from the waterfront. Pick your meal from a selection of fresh fish, straight from the harbour. ⓐ 15 Riga Fereou
ⓣ 22420 21795 ⓛ 12.00–23.00

Pak ££ ❻ Authentic North Indian food served as spicy as you like. The restaurant is on a quiet street and has a nice terrace surrounded by delicately carved Indian doorways. ⓐ A. Patakou Street ⓣ No phone
ⓛ 17.00–24.00

Taverna Therma ££ ❼ One of the best fish restaurants in Kos, with a constantly changing menu according to the daily catch.
ⓐ Down by the hot springs at Psalidi (remember to bring your swimsuit!)
ⓣ 69770 70744 ⓛ 10.00–22.00

The Wolves' Nest ££ ❽ A friendly Greek taverna in the backstreets of Kos serving great local dishes and some international options. ⓐ Bouboulinas ❸ 22420 21737 ❹ 10.00–23.00

Anatolia Hamam £££ ❾ A beautiful restaurant, housed in the ancient hamam (bath-house). Specialities include rabbit *stifado* (stew) and pork fillet with plum sauce. The wine list is impressive and there is a children's menu too. ⓐ 3 Nissiriou (behind Diagoras Square) ❸ 22420 28323 ❹ 09.00–24.00

Otto e Mezzo £££ ❿ The garden terrace of this top Italian restaurant makes a lovely setting for a romantic meal. Specialities include fresh pasta, grilled meats and mouthwatering homemade cakes. ⓐ 21 Apelou Ifestou ❸ 22420 20069 ❹ 09.00–24.00; food served from 12.00

Platanos £££ ⓫ Imaginative Greek and Mediterranean dishes served in a grand Italian-era building near the ancient agora and with good views of Hippocrates' plane tree. ⓐ Town centre ❸ 22420 28991 ⓦ www.platanos-kos.gr

⬥ Take a coffee break in Eleftherias Square

To Petrino £££ ⑫ This charming candlelit garden restaurant is known for its excellent *mezedes*, stuffed vegetables, and seafood dishes.
ⓐ Theologou Square ⓣ 22420 27251 ⓛ 18.00–24.00

AFTER DARK

Apoplous ⑬ This up market bouzouki club has a resident orchestra and singers, various guest artists from mainland Greece are often invited. ⓐ G Papandreou Street, Psalidi ⓣ 22420 21916 ⓛ 24.00–05.00

Charisma Club ⑭ One of the better party bars in Kos Town
ⓐ Bar Street ⓣ 22420 25298 ⓛ 20.30–04.00 (to 06.00 Fri & Sat)

Haman ⑮ Bar set in an old Turkish bath, with occasional live music, plus Greek music and chart-topping hits. ⓐ 1 Akti Koundourioti
ⓣ 22420 24938 ⓛ 21.00–04.00 (disco from 24.00)

SHOPPING
The **central fruit and vegetable market** (ⓛ 06.00–23.00 Mon–Sat, 10.00–14.00 & 19.00–23.00 Sun) on Eleftherias Square also sells honey, Greek Delight and nuts. The shops surrounding the market sell ceramics, embroidery and other souvenirs. Drinks and wine are inexpensive in Greece and there are many different shops throughout town. Other useful shops are:
Hercules For hand-painted ceramics, candles, soaps, shells and sponges. ⓐ 20 Apellou Street
Kos Sport Centre Large shops with sports articles. ⓐ 10 Xanthou
News stand For international newspapers, magazines, books and maps on Kos. ⓐ 2 Riga Ferrou
Pure Silver and Argentum For good quality jewellery.
ⓐ 1 & 7 Apellou Street
Ti Amo Music Modern and traditional Greek music.
ⓐ 4 Al. Ipsilandou Street

Tingaki

Located on the northern coast of Kos, Tingaki (also known as Tigaki) is a mere 15-minute drive from the nightlife of Kos Town, but offers a more relaxed pace for those who prefer quiet evenings and a peaceful environment. Cycling is a great way to get around, and there are safe bike paths leading to Kos Town. With its sheltered Blue Flag beach, Tingaki is also the perfect destination for families.

Once a humble fishing village, Tingaki is now a small, pleasant resort with a handful of medium-sized hotels and attractive apartment blocks scattered amongst fields along the coast. Its long, tree-fringed beach of coarse, white sand is one of the finest on the island, with sunbeds and parasols supplied, and an excellent variety of watersports. The outlines of Kalymnos and Pserimos islands and Turkey's Bodrum Peninsula on the horizon provide a spectacular backdrop.

Tingaki is also the perfect base from which to explore inland, where the countryside is unexpectedly lush and fertile, and its narrow lanes bright with flowers and pretty houses. Take the winding mountain road through the cluster of five villages, collectively known as Asfendiou, where the whitewashed houses clinging to the slopes of Mount Dikaio are sheltered from the sun by forests, fruit and walnut groves. The village of Zia has the best views and also makes a good lunch stop, though at times the crowds can be tiresome.

THINGS TO SEE & DO

Cycling
Hire a bike for the day to explore the surrounding countryside or to cycle into Kos Town. If you're feeling really energetic, you could head inland to the Asklepion or to some of the island's beautiful mountain villages. Both **Nikos** (📞 22420 68380 🕐 08.00–22.00) and **Manolis** (📞 22420 69230 🕐 10.00–19.00) rent bicycles and scooters.

Go-karting

Providing fun for all the family, **Christos Go-Karting** track has special mini-karts for children as young as two. There's also a small bar serving snacks.

ⓐ Marmari main road ❶ 22420 68184 ❶ 09.30–23.00

Horse riding

Lessons and guided riding excursions for children and adults of all levels are available from the Marmari Riding Centre (ⓐ halfway between Tingaki and Marmari ❶ 69441 04446) and Alfa Horse (ⓐ Amaniou village ❶ 22420 41908). You can opt for a trot along the beach or treks into the mountains.

Mountain villages

The unspoilt Asfendiou villages – **Amaniou**, **Evangelistria**, **Lagoudi**, **Pyli** and **Zia** – clustered on the fertile slopes of **Mount Dikaio**, provide a rare glimpse of rural island life before tourism took hold. Evangelistria is especially picturesque, with its low, whitewashed houses, attractive Byzantine church and popular taverna. Zia, the highest village on Kos, is more developed, with several excellent restaurants and souvenir shops. The countryside is popular for walking and horse riding. One footpath leads from the village to the summit of Mount Dikaio (846 m/2,775 ft), passing the Kefalovrysi church – a three-hour climb.

SHOPPING

Useful shops in Tingaki include **Katras Supermarket and Tourist Shop** (ⓐ Main Square ❶ 08.30–22.30), a one-stop convenience store at the heart of the resort for food, drink, papers and magazines, books, beachwear, buckets and spades, and souvenirs. On the outskirts, **Konstantinos hypermarket** (❶ Mon–Sat 08.00–22.30) is especially handy for those in self-catering. It also stocks leatherware, clothing and souvenirs. For reasonably priced jewellery, try **The Gold Shop** (ⓐ Main road ❶ 10.00–19.00).

Watersports

A wide variety of watersports is available on the beach near Tingaki Square, including water-skiing, sailing, windsurfing and pedaloes.

Watersports Xtreme £ ⓐ Kos Town beach ① 69445 74347 ② 10.00–17.00

TAKING A BREAK

Asfendiou £ This charming taverna in picturesque Evangelistria serves a simple menu of hearty local dishes, such as stuffed cabbage leaves or beef stew. Excellent value. ⓐ Evangelistria main square ① 22420 68679 ② 08.00–20.30

Pastry shop £ All the ingredients for a beach or mountain picnic; fresh bread, sandwiches, salads, pastries, crêpes and more. ⓐ Beach road ① 08.00–04.00 ② 08.00–23.00

Tingaki Restaurant £ Traditional taverna, à la carte or set menus. ⓐ Tingaki main square ① 22420 69951 ② 09.00–23.00

Artemis ££ Greek and international food with a view of the beach. There's a handy picture menu to help you decide. ⓐ Beachfront ① 22420 41600 ② 08.30–03.00

Olympia Taverna ££ The only restaurant in Zia without a view but reputedly one of the best tavernas on the island. The stuffed vine leaves and sausage and pepper stew are especially recommended. ⓐ Zia (upper quarter of the village) ① 22420 69121 ⓦ www.olympia-zia.gr ② 09.30–01.00

Plori ££ With wonderful sea views and fairy lights at night, this restaurant specialises in fish but also offers meat, pasta and other dishes. ⓐ Tingaki ① 22420 69686 ② 12.00–23.00

AFTER DARK

Ipanema £ A small cocktail bar with comfortable open-air seating and a quiet atmosphere. Drinks and snacks. ⓐ Main road ⓣ 10.00–02.00

Memories Bar £ Very friendly bar run by three brothers. Great music from the DJ. ⓐ Main road ⓣ 09.00–01.00

Weekends ££ A modern and popular grill house serving sizzling lunches and dinners before transforming into a funky cocktail bar at night, complete with DJs. Inside the mall just west of Tingaki square.
ⓐ Mall complex ⓣ 22420 68267 ⓛ 10.00–03.00

Marmari & Mastichari

The two fishing villages of Marmari and Mastichari on the north coast of Kos have been developed into peaceful, spacious seaside resorts. Both have broad, sandy beaches backed by sand dunes, and various shops, tavernas and bars, attracting couples and families in search of relaxation and a taste of traditional Greece.

The highlight of Marmari is undoubtedly its magnificent Blue Flag beach of golden sand and shingle. Windsurfing is popular here, and there is also horse riding and go-karting on the outskirts of the resort.

Mastichari is probably the least developed of the northern shore resorts. Its beach is sandy and stretches for miles, with the small, secluded beach of **Troulos** just 1 km ($^1/_2$ mile) to the east, reached by a dirt track. Village life centres on the fishing harbour, lined with the tiny fishing *caiques* which provide fresh fish on the tables of the dozen or so tavernas. It is also an important ferry port for **Kalymnos**, the island of the

● *Marmari's popular beach*

> ## SHOPPING
>
> In Mastichari, try **Gitonia** (☎ 22420 59246 🕒 08.30–23.00) for herbs, hand-carved wood, pottery, carpets and Greek music; **Ira & Pia** (☎ 22420 59108 🕒 09.00–22.30) for traditional gold and silverware; and **Mini-Market Australia** for Greek wines and general provisions. On the outskirts of Marmari is the **Konstantinos hypermarket** (🕒 08.00–22.30 Mon–Sat). For gifts, **Art Gallery Pyli** (🅐 Just behind Pyli village square ☎ 22420 41745) makes exclusive silver and gold jewellery, while **The Mermaid**, opposite, sells striking ceramics.

sponge fishermen, with boats sailing there several times a day, as well as to the tiny nearby island of **Pserimos**.

Marmari and Mastichari are popular with both walkers and cyclists eager to explore the island's hinterland. The charming mountain village of **Pyli**, centred around a tiny square with appealing craft shops and restaurants makes a good lunchtime destination. Three kilometres (2 miles) to the north and perched precariously on a craggy outcrop is **Paleo Pyli**, once the ancient capital of Kos. Now all that remains is a ruined Byzantine castle containing the 11th-century church of Ypapanti (Presentation).

THINGS TO SEE & DO

Basilica

Take a walk to the western end of Mastichari beach to see the remains of a 5th-century basilica, Áyious Ioánnis.

Lido Waterpark

Here you'll find 1,200 m (4,000 ft) of slides, black holes, wave pools, a lazy river and much more to keep both children and adults happy. There's a restaurant and bar on site, too. Ask for the free shuttle bus from Kos and Tingaki. 🅐 Mastichari-Kos road ☎ 22420 59241 🅦 www.lidowaterpark.com 🕒 10.00–19.00 ❶ Admission charge

Windsurfing

The **Fanatic Board Centre** at the western end of the resort rents out wetsuits, boards and other windsurfing equipment, as well as providing lessons for beginners. @ Marmari beach

TAKING A BREAK

El Greco £ This popular beach restaurant serves everything from cooked breakfasts to speciality barbecued steaks and swordfish.
@ Mastichari beach ☎ 22420 59112 ⏰ 08.30–24.00

Horizon £ A pleasant beachside café serving coffee, baguettes and other snacks during the day, and a good spot for sunset and cocktails by night.
@ Mastichari beach path ☎ 22420 59190 ⏰ 10.00–02.00

Saloon Bar £ Western-style snack bar and great cocktails (happy hour 19.00–22.00). @ Mastichari beach ☎ 22420 59318 ⏰ 09.00–02.00

● *The local fishing fleet brings a touch of colour to the harbour*

Kali Kardia ££ A fish restaurant on the harbourfront. The grilled octopus and the fresh fish platter are both highly recommended.
ⓐ Mastichari harbour ⓣ 22420 59289 ⓛ 06.30–01.00

O Makis ££ Hidden in a back street just behind the harbour, a locals' restaurant noted for its *mezedes* and reasonably priced fresh fish.
ⓐ Mastichari ⓣ 22420 59061 ⓛ 09.00–23.00

AFTER DARK

Marmari has no nightlife to speak of; however, Mastichari does have some good options.

Images A calm cocktail bar along the main road near the beach.
ⓐ Marmari, main road ⓣ 22420 41950 ⓛ 19.00–05.00

Number One A popular bar with Sky TV, several international draught beers and music from the 1960s–80s. ⓐ Mastichari, near Vios bar
ⓣ 69784 64439 ⓛ 19.30–02.00

Vios A party bar set beneath the trees, with cocktails and loud music at night and snacks served during the day. ⓐ Mastichari, main road
ⓣ 22420 59330 ⓛ 12.00–04.00

Kardamena

Gently shelving white sands and an unruffled sea make Kardamena (pronounced 'Car-dam-ena') an ideal family resort, but the town really comes alive after the children have gone to bed. You can relax in one of the harbourfront restaurants, then tour the nightspots strung out along the edge of the bay where the entertainment ranges from big-screen TV to drinking challenges, dancing and karaoke.

Kardamena is the second-largest and fastest-growing package resort on Kos, and especially popular with young Brits wanting a taste of home abroad. With its lively atmosphere, jam-packed beach and dazzling neon lights, it is hard to believe this former tiny fishing village was once known for its beauty and serenity. Today it remains attractive, but it is now known for its continuous nightlife, attracting young people from all over Europe to its abundant bars, discos and clubs.

The resort's sand-and-shingle beach runs the length of the resort and is always packed by day. Watersports are popular, especially water-skiing, windsurfing and parasailing. And for those who prefer to stay on dry land, there's go-karting 3 km (2 miles) east of the resort. (📞 22420 92065 🕐 11.00–23.00), sunbathing, and plenty of opportunities for walking and cycling.

BEACHES

The Aqua Sports centres on **Kardamena beach** offer parasailing, water-skiing and windsurfing, etc. There are several swimming pools including Kool Pool, Harriet Pool and Blue Lagoon.

Buses run several times a day (from the taxi rank) to **Paradise Beach**, a beautiful expanse of white sand. At one end it is known as **Bubble Beach** because of the rising bubbles of gas, caused by volcanic activity.

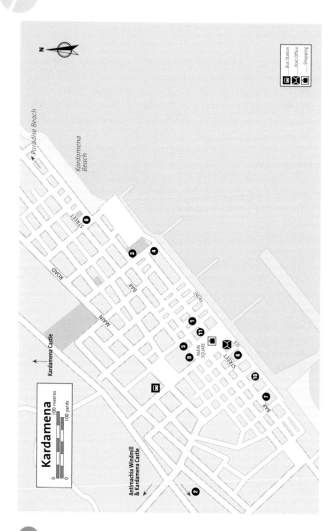

Kardamena

THINGS TO SEE & DO

Antimachia Windmill

The airport at Antimachia will already be familiar to visitors; but don't miss the nearby village with the only working windmill on the island.
🕐 10.00–18.00

Boat trips

There are daily cruises to Nisyros island to visit the active volcano (page 89), day trips to Paradise Beach (page 78), fishing trips or a half-day outings in small day-boats to the tiny island of San Antonio for keen swimmers and snorkellers.

Cycling

On the main road near the taxi rank, **On Yer Bike** and **Bill** (☎ 22420 92273) have a selection of bikes, mopeds and quads for hire.

🔺 Take a ferry from Kardamena to Kefalos for the day

Kardamena Castle

High on a hill to the north of the village, you will see the ancient ruins of Kardamena Castle – a fabulous two-hour walk inland for the energetic, with a breathtaking panorama to reward your efforts. To find the start of the trail, walk eastwards from Starlight disco for 700 m (765 yds). Turn left at the crossroads and, after 500 m (550 yds), you will see a paved path on your right signed to the castle.

TAKING A BREAK

Aramis £ ❶ French and Greek food in a roof-garden setting. Try one of the unusual sauces. Children's and vegetarian menus.
ⓐ One street back from the waterfront ❶ 22420 92056 ❶ 18.00–23.00

Chrisopoulos £ ❷ A delightful blue-and-white taverna on the western edge of town, serving delicious home-made daily specials.
ⓐ Kardamena beach ❶ 22420 91235 ❶ 09.00–18.00

Ellie's Carvery £ ❸ Roasts and other British comfort food including pies, steaks, desserts and salads, all at great prices.
ⓐ Kardamena centre ❶ 22420 92550 ❶ 17.00–23.00, from 14.00 Sun

Alexander ££ ❹ A corner restaurant overlooking the harbour and serving good Greek and international food. You can select your own

SHOPPING

The streets in Kardamena are unnamed but most shops are near the waterfront. **Louis supermarket** sells groceries and alcohol at reasonable prices, and the cream cakes and home-made ice cream at the bakery in the main square are delicious. **Flavours bakery** in the Square (❶ 24 hrs) is a good source of midnight snacks. **Watermelon** and **Passadena** have clothes for all ages, while jewellery can be bought from **Nastos Napoleon** or **Enigma**.

lobster from the tanks here. ⓐ Kardamena centre ⓣ 69322 86012
ⓛ 09.00–24.00

Avli ££ ❺ Sit in the lovely garden and sample the best traditional
Greek fare that Kardamena has to offer. ⓐ Central square ⓣ 22420 92100
ⓦ www.avlirestaurant.gr ⓛ 17.00–24.00

Scala Roof Garden ££ ❻ Considered one of the best restaurants in
Kardamena. Roof-garden, sea view, delicious Greek and Mediterranean
cuisine. ⓐ Harbour ⓣ 22420 92444 ⓛ 08.00–24.00

AFTER DARK

Gum Tree Pub ❼ A mad, Australian-run beach bar serving a good
selection of beer (served very cold) and cheap fishbowls. There's a pool
table, beach service and happy hour from 20.00–22.00. ⓐ Harbourfront
ⓣ 69451 32190 ⓛ 11.00–03.00

The Rok ❽ A busy bar that's open 24 hours (it doesn't even have doors
to close!) serving snacks, barbecue and pub grub (**££**) by day, beer and
cocktails by night when the DJ gets the crowd moving. ⓐ Harbourfront
ⓣ No phone ⓛ 24 hrs

Stone Roses ❾ Set in an elegant building on the main square, the DJs
at this bar play Indie music to a happy party crowd. Guinness® and local
beers on tap. ⓐ Main square ⓛ 11.00–03.00

Starlight ❿ The biggest club in town, home of the Hedkandi
clubnights, foam parties, and a regular venue for visiting big-name UK
and foreign DJs. ⓐ Main road ⓣ 22420 91313 ⓦ www.starlightclub.gr

Status ⓫ Air-conditioned disco club with a large dance floor. House
music and foam parties. ⓐ Town centre ⓣ 22420 91645 ⓛ 24.00–04.00
(until 06.00 at weekends)

Kefalos

The atmosphere of old Greece awaits you in the peaceful village of Kefalos, set on a hillside at the southernmost point of Kos, dominated by the imposing windmill of Papavasillis, and overlooking the spectacular long curve of Kamari Bay with its quiet beach and crystal-clear, shallow waters. Along the shoreline is Kefalos's newest beach resort – a long, thin development, with hotels spread along the beach road and a wide selection of traditional-style bars and tavernas.

In contrast to the busy resorts of Kos Town and Kardamena, Kefalos is gentle and relaxing, with some of the best beaches on the island. The main sand-and-shingle beach runs the entire length of **Kamari Bay** and overlooks a pretty island with the ancient church of **Aghios Nikolaos**. Here you will find plenty to occupy you, whether you fancy trying your hand at windsurfing, sailing, parascending or water-skiing, enjoying a fun trip on a pedalo, or simply lazing the hours away on a sun-lounger.

Should you tire of Kamari Bay, small boats shuttle visitors daily from Kefalos harbour to further sandy beaches just round the headland, with idyllic names such as **Paradise**, **Hawaii**, **Magic** and **Bubble Beach** (named for the volcanic gas vents in the tidal stream which turn the sea into an open-air jacuzzi). Alternatively, there are daily fishing trips; or excursions to **Nisyros** (page 89) and the **Turkish mainland** (page 82).

THINGS TO SEE & DO

Boat trips

Boats leave for Nisyros twice weekly; otherwise you can join a daily cruise to Paradise and Maros beaches. Reservations at any travel agent.

Watersports

The Club Med Watersports Centre (☎ 69776 93684 ◷ 10.30–18.00) opposite St Nicholas island has a wide variety of sports to choose from. The windsurf rental is for Club Med guests only. Further south, Baywatch

🔺 *The remains of a 6th-century basilica along Aghios Stefanos beach*

Watersports (☎ 69723 90421 🕐 10.00–18.00) has two outlets with jet-skis, parasailing, banana rides and more.

TAKING A BREAK

Faros ££ Alongside the fishing harbour, the 'Lighthouse' serves copious quantities of fresh fish as well as international dishes. ⓐ Kamari harbour ☎ 22420 71240 🕐 09.00–23.00

Stamatia ££ This traditional-style taverna, romantically situated on the beach, serves wholesome Greek cuisine. Try the *bekri mese* (pork with mushrooms, garlic, mustard and wine) or the Greek plate (tomatoes and paprika stuffed with minced meat). ⓐ Kamari Bay road ☎ 22420 71245 🕐 09.00–23.00

Taverna Katerina ££ Hidden down a bumpy track at Aghios Stefanos Beach (to the east of Kamari Bay), this delightful taverna serves fantastic fresh fish. Well worth the detour. ⓐ Aghios Stefanos Beach, Kefalos ⓣ 22420 71513 ⓛ 08.00–22.00

The Great Aussie BBQ ££ Cook your own choice of meat on the outdoor chargrill barbecue here. For a special gourmet treat, order yourself the surf 'n' turf platter (sirloin steak with prawns and lobster medallions in a cream sauce). ⓐ Main road ⓣ 22420 71734 ⓛ 08.00–24.00

AFTER DARK

B52 Choose from over 40 cocktails at this bar near Sydney's. There's cosy seating with beach views, a pool table, sports on TV and daily DJs, too. ⓐ Kamari Bay road ⓣ 22420 71395 ⓛ 09.00–06.00

Opa-Opa This candlelit cocktail bar overlooking the beach is surely one of the island's most romantic haunts for an early evening drink. Later most evenings, there is a live DJ and dance music. ⓐ Main road ⓣ 69376 57672 ⓛ 09.00–02.00

Popeye's An English bar with a friendly atmosphere, draught beer, pool tables, internet, Sky TV and films shown at 22.00. The Survivor disco (from 24.00–06.00) is at the back, with a DJ playing dance music, Greek on Saturdays. ⓐ Main road ⓣ 22420 71579 ⓛ 18.00–03.30

Sydney A lively seafront bar halfway along the bay, with a pool, sports on TV, great steaks and other food (**££**), and DJs playing every night to a happy crowd. ⓐ Kamari bay road ⓣ 22420 71286 ⓦ www.sydneybar.com ⓛ 10.00–03.00

ⓞ *Excursion boats around Symi (see page 95)*

Marmaris

You will already have been tantalised by glimpses of the Turkish mainland from Greece – this is your chance to see it at first hand. Several fast ferries and hydrofoils leave Rhodes harbour every day, taking 45–90 minutes to reach Marmaris, so there's plenty of time to take in the sights, do a bit of shopping and have a meal in a seafront *lokanta*.

Kaleiç is the diminutive, but picturesque old quarter of Marmaris. The castle dates from the 11th century but was enlarged by Süleyman the Magnificent in 1522 during his campaign to conquer Rhodes. The bazaar, a labyrinth of alleyways behind the promenade, is one of the liveliest on the Mediterranean coast. You can pick up some real bargains here, so long as you barter.

Visitors require an exit stamp on their passports to visit Turkey, so it is best to book through an agent who knows the correct procedures.

THINGS TO SEE & DO

Atlantis Aquapark
This attraction in Uzunyalı, just beyond Long Beach, is perfect for adults and children of all ages, with numerous convoluted water slides and rides. Hop on the turquoise dolmus (minibus) to get there.

ⓐ 3 Siteler Mah. 212 Sok, Uzunyalı ⓣ +90 252 411 04 61
ⓦ www.marmarisinfo.com/waterpark ⓒ 10.00–18.00 ⓘ Admission charge

> ### SHOPPING
> Reliable shops within the Bazaar complex include:
> **Paradise Carpets** For rugs and kilims. ⓐ 42 Sokak 15
> **Goldium** For jewellery. ⓐ Yeni Çarsi Sokak 24
> **Gersu Leather** For leatherware. ⓐ Yeni Çarsi Sokak 24
> **Iris** For perfumes and cosmetics. ⓐ Tepe Mah 47
> Don't forget to bargain. It is expected – even in shops.

Friday Market

Villagers converge on Marmaris once a week, clogging up the roads and back streets with carts laden with produce. Definitely an experience not to be missed.

AFTER DARK

Haç Mustafa Sokagi, universally known as 'Bar Street', is in the centre of Marmaris. Here dancing continues until 05.00 at the height of the season, but many bars are open during the day too.

● *Pop over to Turkey for a bit of shopping*

Bodrum

Until a few years ago, Bodrum was a remote fishing village. Now, it is the undisputed tourist hotspot of the Turkish coast, a bustling, cosmopolitan resort with an unrivalled choice of shops and restaurants, yet it still retains the character of a traditional market town. It is also one of the prettiest towns on the Aegean coast, a mass of sugar-cube-shaped, whitewashed houses clustered around a dazzling blue bay. You can take a day trip from Kos harbour to Bodrum – the boat takes just an hour to get there.

Known in ancient times as Halicarnassus, Bodrum was the birthplace of Herodotus, the 'father of written history', and the site of the tomb of King Mausolus, one of the Seven Wonders of the World. Little remains today of ancient Bodrum apart from a few scattered ruins (including a well-preserved amphitheatre) and the spectacular medieval castle built by the Knights of St John, which guards the entrance to the harbour where elegant yachts crowd the palm-lined waterfront and the chic marina.

The reputation of Bodrum's boatyards dates back to ancient times and craftsmen can still be seen building traditional wooden boats, including the *gulet* (motor-yacht) with its distinctive broad beam and rounded stern, today mostly used for pleasure trips along the scenic Bodrum peninsula.

THINGS TO SEE & DO

Aquapark

Turkey's biggest water fun-park with 24 water slides, numerous restaurants and an action-packed programme of poolside entertainment. Be sure to try the Kamikaze slide, the Twin Twister and the Big Hole!

ⓐ Dedeman Aquapark, Ortakent road (on Bodrum's western outskirts)
ⓣ +90 252 368 6161 ⓦ www.depark.com.tr ⓛ 10.30–18.30
ⓘ Admission charge

⬤ *Explore Bodrum Castle and its towers*

SHOPPING

Leatherware, cotton goods, jewellery, carpets, natural sponges and local blue-glass beads are among the best buys in the friendly little shops that line the narrow streets of Bodrum. The bustling **bazaar** (clothing, carpets and fabrics on Tuesdays; fruit and vegetables on Fridays) is full of excellent bargains, but you must haggle for a good price. Be careful when purchasing gold. It is priced by weight and the lowest carat is 14. Gold is not hallmarked in Turkey, so you need to get a certificate showing its weight and what carat it is. If the shop is not forthcoming with the necessary paperwork, think twice before buying.

Babil Center A sweet-smelling store containing Turkish Delight, herbs, spices, apple tea, honey, nuts and coffee. ❸ Kumbahçe Camii Alti (entrance in Uçkuyular Street)

Dalyanci Galeri The gaily coloured, handmade pottery here makes ideal gifts. ❸ Cumhuriyet Caddesi, Alim Bey Pasaji 55

There are also **Duty Free** shops in the harbour where you can purchase cigarettes and perfumes.

Bodrum Castle

The medieval Castle of St Peter is a magnificent example of 15th-century Crusader architecture, built on the site of an ancient acropolis by the Knights of Rhodes. It has recently been converted into a stunning **Museum of Underwater Archaeology**, with treasures salvaged from shipwrecks dating back to the Bronze Age.

🕐 08.30–12.00 & 13.00–17.00 Tues–Sun ❶ Admission charge

Turkish Bath

Treat yourself to an authentic Turkish Bath at the **Bodrum Hamam**. There are separate sections for men and women and massages (oil or scrub) are also available.

❸ Cevat Sakir Caddesi, Fabrika Sokak ❶ 00 90 252 313 4129
🕐 06.00–24.00

TAKING A BREAK

Lokanta £ ❶ The Turkish equivalent of a *tapas* bar. No need to worry if you don't speak Turkish because all the dishes are on display and all you have to do is point at what you want. ⓐ Cumhuriyet Caddesi 115 ① 00 90 252 316 8383 ⓛ 11.00–24.00

Epsilon ££ ❷ An atmospheric restaurant specialising in both international and Turkish dishes, including a wide variety of tasty *mezedes* (appetisers). ⓐ Türkkuyusu Mah. Keleş Çikmazi ① 00 90 252 313 2964 ⓛ 11.00–24.00

Secret Garden £££ ❸ Fantastic fine dining in a romantic garden near the marina. The English-run restaurant serves Turkish and Mediterranean dishes, but leave space for the homemade desserts. ⓐ 20 Danacı Sokak, behind Marina Vista Hotel ① 00 90 252 313 1641 ⓛ 12.00–24.00

● *Bodrum offers an unrivalled choice of shops and restaurants*

Nisyros

This seductive island was formed millions of years ago by volcanic activity and the giant crater, Stephanos, is still the main attraction for visitors. You'll also see olives, figs, lemons and almonds all growing in abundance on the terraced slopes above Mandraki, the island's tiny port where life has changed little in the last 2,000 years. Excursion boats run regularly between Kos harbour and Nisyros, taking around an hour to get there.

The volcano has been intermittently active for centuries, and although the last major eruption was in 1888, continuous seismic activity has now been recorded for more than two years. The largest of five craters, Stephanos measures an astonishing 300 m (328 yds) across. You'll need strong shoes for the 22 m (72 ft) descent which, incidentally, is made at your own risk. There is an overpowering stench of sulphur dioxide (think rotten eggs) but it's a price worth paying for this once-in-a-lifetime opportunity.

THINGS TO SEE & DO

Mandraki

Mandraki, which is the main port of Nisyros, is a delightful town of whitewashed houses. Its narrow alleys are overlooked by two ruined castles and one of several religious centres on the island – **Spilliani Monastery** (🕐 10.30–17.00), with its striking solid gold altar. If you think the 120 steps up to the monastery are hard work, spare a thought for the womenfolk of Mandraki who, on 25 August each year, climb them on their knees as a gesture of reverence! The bird's-eye view from the top makes the climb worthwhile.

Pali

Just 4 km (2½ miles) from Mandraki, this picturesque fishing port is popular with visitors for its sandy beaches and wonderful tavernas.

TAKING A BREAK

Hellinis Taverna £ This friendly waterfront taverna serves highly recommended Greek, international and fresh fish dishes. ⓐ Waterfront, Pali 🕘 08.00–23.00

Tony's Taverna £ This Australian-owned taverna is ideal for a light lunch by the water's edge. ⓐ Waterfront, Mandraki 🕔 22420 31509 🕘 08.00–24.00

Fabrika £–££ The best ouzeri in town, a simple, small bar with convivial owners and great drinks. ⓐ Mandraki harbour 🕔 19.00–22.00; closed Thur

Aphrodite ££ Reputedly the best taverna in Pali, known for its fresh fish and meat dishes, served with Rhodian wine straight from the barrel. ⓐ Waterfront, Pali 🕘 07.00–24.00

SHOPPING

Shopping on Nisyros is always a pleasure. In Mandraki, look out for **Artin Caracasian**'s photographic studio (ⓐ On the left-hand side of the main street as you head uphill from the port), where you can purchase magnificent photographs of the island, and the **Sunflower craft shop** (ⓐ On the right-hand side of the main street as you head uphill from the port), which sells delightful pottery, glass and jewellery, some of which uses obsidian, a precious black glass-like stone from neighbouring Yali island that was once used by Hippocrates for his cutting instruments.

Some of the food stores sell the island's delicious speciality, *soumadha* (a milky almond drink), and the tiny village **bakery** in Pali sells crusty brown bread – a rarity in Greece.

Kalymnos

The fourth-largest island in the Dodecanese, Kalymnos (Kalimnos) is famous for the sponges that are sold from the quayside warehouses of Pothia, the busy main port. Here visitors can learn about the colourful history and traditions of the industry and see how the sponges are cleaned and treated. Ferries leave Mastichari and Kos Town daily for Pothia.

Apart from Pothia, the island's other attractions include thermal springs, caverns dripping with stalactites, crumbling Byzantine ruins and numerous coves and beaches, perfect for swimming and sunbathing. The island is also popular for rock-climbing, and there's even a climbing festival every October.

In times gone by, sponge fishermen dived naked and unprotected (sometimes to depths of 75 m/246 ft), weighted with heavy stones and carrying a rope as a lifeline. Today's fishermen wear regulation wetsuits and carry oxygen tanks, but diving remains a hazardous business. Sadly, disease has wreaked havoc among the Mediterranean sponges and the industry has fallen sharply into decline – only a couple of boats now put regularly to sea.

The people of Kalymnos still mark the annual departure of the fishermen, usually just after Orthodox Easter, with an exuberant festival called *Iprogros* (Sponge Week).

SHOPPING

Apart from the stalls selling shells and sponges, try **Kalypso** (🅐 In an alley beside Anastasio bar) for jewellery and pottery, the **Bottle Store** (🅐 On the waterfront) for local wines, and **To Petrino** in Enoria Christou (🅐 Just off the waterfront) for unusual gift ideas.

THINGS TO SEE & DO

Nautical and Folklore Museum

This small but fascinating museum vividly recounts the remarkable history of the island and its heroic sponge divers.
ⓐ Beside the cathedral ⓛ 08.30–13.30; closed Mon ❶ Admission charge

Pothia

Behind the many harbourfront cafés and tavernas of Pothia, the island's capital, lies hidden an original Greek town, totally unspoilt by tourism, with its tiers of multi-coloured houses lining the narrow streets and stepped alleyways. It also boasts one of the four cathedrals of the Dodecanese islands (along with Rhodes, Kos and Karpathos), countless churches and several splendid Venetian-style municipal buildings, which adorn the seafront.

Pserimos

Many excursion boats leaving Kalymnos for Kos stop off for a couple of hours at Pserimos, enabling people to swim in the crystal-clear waters and to enjoy the sandy beach of this idyllic little island.

Vouvalis Mansion

The lovely 19th-century mansion formerly owned by Nikolaos Vouvalis, a wealthy trader and sponge merchant is now a museum with three sumptuous period rooms on display. The dining room is set for a meal on Sheffield plates, and the neo-Baroque living room has a small archaeological collection.
ⓐ Beside the Archaeological Museum ⓣ 08.30–14.00 ❶ Admission fee. A new archaeological museum is due to open in 2008 behind the Vouvalis Mansion.

TAKING A BREAK

Anasis £ A modern bakery café with delicious coffee, pastries, bread, and homemade ice cream for eating on the terrace. ⓐ Main square ⓣ 22430 29992 ⓛ 08.30–23.00

Omilos ££ You will be made welcome at this hospitable restaurant, which serves a variety of local specialities. ⓐ Beside the docks ⓣ 22430 29239 ⓛ 07.00–15.30 & 18.00–24.00

Rempetiko ££ Delicious Greek meals including *mououri* (stuffed lamb), *kavourma* (fried pork) and Kalymnian *mirmizelli* salad. ⓐ Main street, beside the town hall ⓣ 22430 51787 ⓛ 09.00–24.00

🔺 *The traditional preserved settlement of Pothia*

Southern Rhodes

The southwest coast

Take the coastal road from Rhodes Town past the airport and continue through the villages of **Paradissi, Theologos** and **Soroni**, until you reach Kamiros. Set on a hill amidst pine trees, the site of ancient **Kamiros** is one of the three ancient settlements on Rhodes, and the agora (square), residential districts and acropolis constitute one of the best-preserved classical towns in Greece (🕒 08.00–19.10 Tues–Sun ❶ Admission charge).

Follow the coastal road to the fishing village of Kamiros Skala and then turn inland into the rugged mountains, with glimpses of the Knights' 16th-century hillside fortress to the right. Picturesque **Kritinia** is worth a stop, before continuing to **Siana**, a delightful village where time stands still – the hands on the church clock are painted on. Shop here for thyme honey and *souma* (a local liquor), before heading on to **Monolithos**. This village takes its name from the 250 m (820 ft) high rock (*mono* meaning 'one', *lithos* meaning 'rock') just beyond the village, with an ancient castle perched precariously at its summit. From here, the road snakes down to a small, rocky beach, a pleasant stop for a dip in the sea.

Head back towards Rhodes Town via Empona, noted for wine and folk dancing. Visit Emery wine factory on the outskirts of the village for visits and tastings (🕒 09.00–16.30), and **Alexandris Wines**, which is located in the basement of a house. Ask a local for directions!

The southeast coast

Moni Thari (Thari Monastery), 10 km (6 miles) inland from Lardos, is open to the public (🕒 10.00–18.00) and really worth a visit. See page 55 for more information.

Further south, Prassonissi or 'Leek Island' marks Rhodes' southernmost extremity, where the Aegean Sea meets the Mediterranean – a paradise for windsurfers. From May to September you can stroll across the sandy causeway that links Prassonissi to the rest of Rhodes.

Symi

Cameras click furiously as the excursion boats round the headland into Yialos, the main port of the spectacularly beautiful island of Symi. Rising above the harbour are tiers of elegant, neo-classical mansions, coloured predominantly ochre with blue, green or orange shutters. It takes approximately an hour and a half to get here by boat from Mandraki harbour.

BEACHES

Local taxis will take you to the tiny fishing hamlet of **Pedi**, the nearest sandy beach, and boat-taxis run to **Nimborio** or to the more secluded beaches on the eastern coast, including **Aghia Marina** and **Aghios Georgios**.

THINGS TO SEE & DO

Panormitis

The delightful little harbour is dominated by the monastery of St Michael the Archangel and its gaily painted bell tower. The church, illuminated only by the gleam of lamps and incense burners, contains the resplendent armour-clad figure of St Michael. The monastic museum contains miniature ships, wax dolls, icons by Fabergé, and a beautifully fashioned mother-of-pearl crib, as well as an assortment of rural and domestic bric-a-brac. Pilgrims sometimes stay in the monastery overnight, occupying the numbered rooms off the main courtyard.

SHOPPING

Buy painted icons in the **monastery shop** at Panormitis and sponges from the **Aegean Sponge Centre** in Yialos. **Harbour stalls** sell honey, olives, oils and boxes of herbs and spices.

Yialos

A flight of 375 steps lead from the harbour to the old town of **Chorio**, a maze of winding alleys and typical village houses. There are wonderful views, and the church contains a mosaic floor depicting a mermaid enticing seamen to their doom. Look out for the 19th-century pharmacy, complete with apothecary jars, and the folklore museum housed in an elegant mansion, with a reconstructed interior of a traditional Symiot house (ⓐ Tues–Sun 10.00–14.00 ❶ Admission charge). If you follow the signs up to Kastro, you will find an acropolis, knights' castle and traces of prehistoric walls.

TAKING A BREAK

Tholos £ Magnificent harbour views. Menu includes Greek, international and daily-changing fish dishes. ⓐ On the waterfront (beyond the Harani boatyard) ❶ 22460 72033 ❷ 11.00–15.00 & 19.00–23.00

Vapori £ Friendly bar in Yialos harbour, with an excellent choice of snacks, drinks and cocktails. ⓐ At the start of the 375 steps up to Chorio ❶ 22460 72082 ❷ 08.00–01.00

Ellenikon ££ A wine-lover's paradise, this restaurant stocks over 150 Greek wines, and dozens bottles line the walls. The waiters can suggest which wine to try with your Greek food. Don't skip the homemade ice cream! ⓐ Main square ❶ 22460 72455 ❷ 09.00–23.00

Mythos ££ The best place to try meze – come with friends, order a selection of plates and try a bit of everything. The cook, Stavros, also makes many other delicious Greek meals. ⓐ Harbourfront ❶ 22460 71488 ❷ 09.00–23.00

❶ *Arched doorway, Lindos*

Food & drink

LOCAL FOOD

Greek cooking uses the freshest ingredients and is nourishing, tasty and filling. As very little produce is imported, dishes are based on local foodstuffs. Vegetarians, however, will find their options fairly limited because even vegetable dishes may be cooked with beef stock. So, although in every resort you will be sure to come across English and international standards, be sure not to miss out on the delicious food that the islands have to offer.

APPETISERS

A typical Greek meal begins with a basket of fresh bread and a selection of *mezedes*. Order several dishes and share them with your friends. The highlights are *horiatiki*, a refreshing salad comprising feta cheese, tomato, cucumber and black olives; *tzatziki* (cucumber yoghurt dip); *taramossaláta* (a paste of cod roe and lemon juice) and *saganaki* (fried cheese fritter). Cheese or spinach pies also make good snacks – try *kopanisti*, a soft, tasty cheese (usually feta, which is made with goat's milk) with red-hot peppers.

MAIN COURSES

Meat is cheap and plentiful. The most succulent dishes include *souvláki* or *shish kebab* – garlic-marinated lamb dressed with onions; *keftedes* – meatballs with mint, onion, eggs and bacon; moussaka – layers of minced lamb with sliced aubergine and bechamel sauce; *kleftiko* – slow-cooked lamb; and *stifado* – beef with onions and tomato sauce. Or you might like to try *dolmades* – vine-leaf parcels stuffed with rice, minced lamb and pine kernels and braised in lemon and olive oil.

Fishermen's catches of red mullet, sole, snapper or sea bream may be brought to your table if you've found a good seaside taverna. Before ordering, remember that fish is sold by weight; establish the price first – a good rule of thumb is that one kilo (2.2 lb) serves four people.

🔻 *Try out some Greek fish dishes*

Prawns, stuffed mussels, fried squid and stewed octopus (often cooked in white wine, with potatoes and tomatoes) are all widely available. Swordfish steaks are also popular, served grilled with lemon, salt and pepper.

If you suddenly become peckish around lunchtime but don't want to sit down to a full meal, *gyros* – doner kebab in pitta bread – or the snack version of *souvláki* – pitta bread filled with meat, tomato and onion – will fill a hole.

DESSERTS

Most Greeks will settle for fresh fruit after a meal – the watermelons are unbelievably juicy – or there are apricots, peaches and grapes. If you have a sweet tooth, try *baklava*, a pastry soaked in honey with almonds and walnuts, *loukoumades*, a kind of honey fritter, or *bougatsa*, a hot pie with a creamy filling of custard and cinnamon. More revitalising on a hot day is yoghurt topped with honey and almonds – delicious!

DRINKS

Soft drinks, like colas and lemonades, are sold everywhere but freshly made orange or lemon juice is more refreshing in hot weather. Mineral water (still or fizzy) is equally thirst-quenching – Greek brands are perfectly safe and acceptable. Outside the hotels, tea generally means hot water and a teabag because Greeks don't generally drink it as we do.

Greek coffee is served in small cups, is strong in flavour, has a treacly texture and leaves a thick sediment. Ask for *gliko* if you like it sweet, *metrio* (medium), or *sketo* (without sugar). If you prefer you can order espresso or instant (ask for Nes). In resorts, cappuccino is increasingly available. And there's nothing more refreshing on a hot day than a *frappé* (iced coffee).

WINE & BEER

The most distinctive Greek wine is *retsina*. Flavoured with pine resin, it takes some getting used to and you may prefer it with lemonade or soda water. *Retsina* is supposed to complement the oil in Greek food, though it is definitely an acquired taste. The best local wines are produced by the Emery and the CAIR companies of Rhodes. Emery's Villaré, a prize-winning dry white, is reputed to be one of the best in Greece. CAIR's offerings also include a light, red table wine, Chevalier de Rhodes. Equally good value are the sparkling wines, Grand-Prix and Brut.

Greek lager is very drinkable and cheaper than imported beer – ask for Mythos or Hellas. The most widely available foreign brands are Heineken, Amstel, Kronenbourg and Budweiser. Specify that you want bottled or draught beer, as cans are often a great deal more expensive.

SPIRITS

The Greek national drink is *ouzo*, an aniseed-flavoured spirit usually drunk as an aperitif. *Ouzo* can be consumed straight, but if you intend to have more than one glass, follow custom and dilute it with water. You may also be offered *raki*, a spirit made from distilled wine, grape skins and pips. Greek brandy is also highly palatable, and available in various strengths and prices, indicated by star ratings (3, 5, 7). The best-known brand, Metaxa, is dark and sweet, but you could also ask for the drier Kamba.

⬤ *A typical Greek salad makes a great starter*

Menu decoder

Here are some of the authentically Greek dishes that you might encounter in tavernas or pastry shops.

Dolmadákia Vine leaves stuffed with rice, onions, dill, parsley, mint and lemon juice

Domátes/piperiés yemistés Tomatoes/peppers stuffed with herb-flavoured rice (and sometimes minced lamb or beef)

Fassólia saláta White beans (haricot, butter beans) dressed with olive oil, lemon juice, parsley, onions, olives and tomato

Lazánia sto fourno Greek lasagne, similar to Italian lasagne, but often including additional ingredients, such as chopped boiled egg or sliced Greek-style sausages

Makaronópita A pie made from macaroni blended with beaten eggs, cheese and milk, baked in puff pastry

Melitzanópita A pie made from baked liquidised aubergines mixed with onions, garlic, breadcrumbs, eggs, mint and parmesan cheese

Melitzanossaláta Aubergine dip made from baked aubergines, liquidised with tomatoes, onions and lemon juice

Moussakás Moussaka, made from fried slices of aubergines, interlayered with minced beef and *béchamel* sauce

Pastítsio Layers of macaroni, haloumi cheese and minced meat (cooked with onions, tomatoes and basil), topped with *béchamel* sauce and baked

Píta me kymá Meat pie made from minced lamb and eggs, flavoured with onions and cinnamon and baked in filo pastry

Saláta horiátiki Country salad (known in England as 'Greek salad'); every restaurant has its own recipe, but the basic ingredients are tomatoes, cucumber, onions, green peppers, black olives, oregano and feta cheese dressed with vinegar, olive oil and oregano

Souvláki Kebab – usually of pork cooked over charcoal

Spanakotyropitákia Cigar-shaped pies made from feta cheese, eggs, spinach, onions and nutmeg in filo pastry

Taramossaláta Cod's roe dip made from puréed potatoes, smoked cod's roe, oil, lemon juice and onion

Tyropitákia Small triangular cheese pies made from feta cheese and eggs in filo pastry

Tzatzíki Grated cucumber and garlic in a dressing of yoghurt, olive oil and vinegar

THE KAFENEION

In Greek villages, the *kafeneion* (café) remains very much a male preserve, although visitors of both sexes will be made welcome. Customers come here to read the paper, debate the issues of the day and play backgammon, as well as to consume *café hellenico* (Greek coffee). This is made by boiling finely ground beans in a special pot with a long handle. Sugar is added during the preparation rather than at the table, so you should order *glyko* (sweet), *metrio* (medium) or *sketo* (no sugar). In summer, try *frappé* (with ice).

Shopping

Rhodes clearly has more shopping opportunities than Kos, owing to its size. On both islands, the vast majority of shops are found in the main towns.

LOCAL SPECIALITIES

Certain villages have their own specialities and you'll find it cheaper to buy on the spot. On Rhodes, Lindos, for example, is famous for pottery, while the stallholders of Siana can't wait to sell you jars of locally produced honey. You can buy wines and liqueurs at wholesale prices from the **Emery Factory** in Embonas or, if it's natural sponges you're after, the shops on Kalymnos will be sure to oblige.

   If you see something you like but aren't happy about the price, try polite negotiation; alternatively, walk away with a disappointed look on your face – there's a good chance the trader will call you back.

JEWELLERY

Gold (usually 18 carat) and silver are priced by weight and can be exceptional value because there's such a small mark-up for the workmanship. Most distinctive is the jewellery inspired by ancient Greek or Byzantine designs.

LEATHER GOODS

The choice includes shoes, thonged sandals, bags, satchels, purses, wallets, belts (check stitching and buckles before leaving the shop). For something more unusual, visit Archangelos on Rhodes to order a pair of distinctive made-to-measure peasant boots which protect against snakes!

HANDICRAFTS & LOCAL PRODUCE

Look out for brightly coloured *kourelia* (rag rugs), ceramics (for example hand-painted vases, plates, cockerels, mock fruit and other novelties), painted glass, gift-wrapped baskets of herbs, oils, hand-painted

🔺 *Greece is a good place to find brightly coloured ceramics*

wooden icons, embroidered linen table-cloths and Greek Delight, along with other gooey sweets.

Little blue and white evil eyes will keep you and your family safe. Onyx chess sets, alabaster classical statuettes and silver theatre masks are popular souvenirs, as are *brikis* which are small metal containers used for boiling Greek coffee – you can buy packets of the coffee in local stores.

Children

Greeks adore children, so having them around presents little problem. The danger is that you will actually be ignored in favour of them. In summer, Greek families stay up until after midnight and let their children run around with their friends on the traffic-free streets. For families with young children, Faliraki (Rhodes) and Kardamena (Kos) are the best beaches; gently shelving, with acres of soft sand and shops nearby. Western coast beaches are great for waves but watch out for currents.

BOAT TRIPS

Children love being on the water, so play pirates for a day by sailing to a remote beach with a picnic, either on an organised trip or by hiring your

● *Keep the children entertained at a water park*

own boat. Sailing trips can also include some sightseeing, watching fish through a glass-bottomed boat, snorkelling, searching for dolphins or fishing. Some snorkelling equipment is provided. These trips are not advisable for very young children. Trips can be booked from the boat operators at the resort harbour, or via your hotel.

CASTLES

Children will love exploring the massive fortifications and castle in Rhodes Town and the smaller castle in Kos Town. The impressive Sound & Light show in Rhodes Town is exciting and spectacular for children too, though not for small ones. The ruined Acropolis in Lindos is great for children and they won't complain about the uphill walk if you let a donkey take the strain. On return to the village you can buy a souvenir photograph. Keep a close eye on your children at all castles as not all dangerous areas are fenced off.

PLAYGROUNDS, KARTING & WATER PARKS

Many resorts have small playgrounds with swings, slides, see-saws and climbing frames (unsupervised). Luna Parks at Kremasti and Trianta on Rhodes are suitable for children up to the age of 12, and for slightly older children the karting tracks on both islands have special go-karts. Finally, the waterparks on Rhodes and Kos are paradise for children (and adults).

VOLCANO

Journey to the island of Nisyros (page 89) to see a real live volcano – a once-in-a-lifetime experience and a good talking point. Watch the steam rise from the crater and feel the sticky surface underfoot.

WATERSPORTS

In the main tourist areas there is no shortage of watersports activities for children, such as pedaloes and canoes. Older children can safely have a first go at windsurfing or scuba diving at one of the licensed schools on the islands. A flag system is in operation on most beaches, and there is usually a lifeguard on duty on the more popular beaches.

Sports & activities

ON THE ISLAND OF RHODES

Golf

Afandou Golf Course is the island's only 18-hole (par 73) championship
golf course and was designed by British golf architect, David Harridine.
It is open 12 months a year and has a clubhouse, bar, changing rooms.
🕿 22410 51256 🅦 www.afandougolfcourse.com
Minigolf can be enjoyed in many of the large resorts. There are excellent
courses at the Olympic Palace Hotel in Ixia (🕿 22410 39790
🕒 10.00–23.00) and Lardos (🕿 22440 44332 🕒 10.00–01.00).

Hiking

One of the best walks is to the top of Profitis Ilias Mountain (altitude
720 m/2,360 ft). The ascent takes around three hours. There's a great
café at the summit serving mountain tea and fresh yoghurt and honey.
Walking tours can be arranged with local guides. For full information,
contact the tourist office or your holiday rep, or get a good map and
go it alone.

Sailing

Rhodes is the busiest centre in the Aegean for yachting. A variety of craft
– bare-boat or crewed, sail or power – is available from companies such
as Kronos Yacht (🕿 22410 78407 🅦 www.kronosyacht.gr). Catamaran
sailing is possible from Faliraki beach.

Snorkelling & diving

At Kalithea Spa – a small bay and lido 4 km (2½ miles) south of Rhodes,
built in the 1920s. Excellent swimming, snorkelling and scuba diving.
Hippocrates drank – and recommended – the healing properties of the
spa waters here. Today the domed pavilions stand abandoned and the
waters have long since dried up.

Turkish baths

Steam or massage away all the holiday excess in one of just two functioning Ottoman-era hamams. Men and women bath separately, and towels are provided. ⓐ Platia Arionos (Rhodes Old Town) 🕐 10.00–18.00 Mon–Fri, 08.00–17.00 Sat; closed Sun

Water Park

Faliraki's waterpark is the biggest in Europe, with dozens of activities to keep you wet, cool and happy. Free bus transfers from Mandraki harbour in Rhodes Town. 🕾 22410 84403 Ⓦ www.water-park.gr 🕐 09.30–19.00

Windsurfing

Conditions on Rhodes, especially in the west of the island, are among the best in the world. For more information, contact Windsurfers' World on Ixia beach. 🕾 22410 24995 Ⓦ www.windsurfersworld.gr or **Pro-Center** in Trianda 🕾 22410 95819 Ⓦ www.procenter-rhodos.com

ON THE ISLAND OF KOS

Watersports, including pedaloes, water-skis and sailboards, are available from stands on the beach in many island resorts. There is also a large choice of sporting activities available on Kos – most are based at hotels. To find out more, visit Ⓦ www.koswatersports.gr/english_about.html

- **Aquapark** ⓐ Lido Waterpark, Mastichari-Kos Road 🕾 22420 59241 Ⓦ www.lidowaterpark.com
- **Ideal Bikes** ⓐ Eth. Antistaseos, Kos Town 🕾 22420 29003
- **Kavas Yachting** ⓐ Kos Marina 🕾 22420 20321 Ⓦ www.kavas.kom
- **Horse riding** ⓐ Marmari Riding Centre (halfway between Tingaki and Marmari 🕾 69441 04446) and Alfa Horse (ⓐ Amaniou village 🕾 22420 41908 Ⓦ www.alfa-horse.com)
- **Tennis** ⓐ Continental Palace, Kos Town 🕾 22420 22737
- **Watersports** ⓐ Club Med Watersports Centre, Kefalos 🕾 69776 93684

Festivals & events

SOME MAIN FESTIVALS

St George's Day
23 April Greeks celebrate the patron saint of shepherds.

Easter This is the greatest festival in Greece – more important than Christmas – almost everything shuts down for three days.

St Panteleimon Day
26 July St Panteleimon (a Christian martyr) is honoured and celebrated in Siana (Rhodes) and on Kalymnos.

Feast of the Assumption
15–23 August One of the largest and most boisterous celebrations in the Dodecanese takes place in Kremasti (Rhodes).

Ochi Day
28 October The most important public holiday celebrated throughout Greece. It commemorates Ioannis Metaxas's (Greek dictator 1936–1941) refusal of Mussolini's ultimatum.

OTHER FESTIVALS
Panegyria (religious festivals) play a large part in Greek culture. Various cultural festivals are held in most towns between late June and early September. Wine festivals are held in autumn.

FOLK CULTURE & MUSIC
Organised folk evenings are the nearest most tourists get to Greek folk culture, but some restaurants have live music and maybe some dancing.

 Backstreets in Rhodes Town

Accommodation

Hotel rates (double room rate with breakfast in high season):
£ = below €75
££ = €75–150
£££ = over €150

Hotels

Rhodes and Kos have hundreds of hotels, offering accommodation in all price classes. Many hotels are only open between May to October, with July and August being the busiest months. It's a good idea to book well ahead for high season, though even then hotels often have a few rooms available for last-minute arrivals.

FALIRAKI

Venezia ££ A stroll or short bus ride away from the beach and the resort centre, but with great views, a pleasant garden and a pool. Both rooms and self-catering apartments. ⓐ 85100 Faliraki ⓣ 22410 85612 ⓦ www.venezia-resort.com ❶ No street name

IXIA

Ixian Grand £££ All-inclusive beach resort hotel near the centre of Ixia. There is a large pool and garden and the beach is in front. ⓐ Ixia Beach, Ixia ⓣ 224210 92944 ⓦ www.theixiangrand.gr

KARDAMENA

Norida Beach ££–£££ This large resort hotel is the best in Kardamena, 5 km (3 miles) from the town centre but with a great pool and beach access. ⓐ Kardamena beach, Kardamena ⓣ 22420 91230 ⓦ www.mitsishotels.com

KOLYMBIA

Memphis Beach ££ A hotel near the beach with pool, animation programme and the town's restaurants and bars a short walk away. ⓐ Beach road, Kolymbia ⓣ 22410 56288

KOS TOWN

Continental Palace ££ Next to the town's busy marina and close to both the beach and the city, the hotel has standard rooms and a lovely pool and garden area. ⓐ G. Papandreou St, Kos Town ⓣ 22420 22737
ⓦ www.continentalpalace.com

LINDOS

Lindos Mare ££–£££ A modern boutique hotel draped over a hill with lifts and a cable car to the beach below. It's 2.5 km (1½ miles) from Lindos village. ⓐ Lindos-Kolymbia road, Lindos ⓣ 22440 31130
ⓦ www.lindosmare.gr

MARMARI

Caravia Beach ££–£££ A recently renovated beachside hotel with all amenities on site; large pools, sunbeds, playgrounds, sports facilities and programmes for children. Shops and restaurants can also be found near the hotel. ⓐ Marmari beach, Marmari ⓣ 22420 41291

MASTICHARI

Neptune £££ A large, top-quality beach resort consisting of small buildings surrounded by various pools and gardens. There are plenty of activities on offer and food is all-inclusive. ⓐ Mastichari beach, Mastichari ⓣ 22420 41480 ⓦ www.neptune.gr

RHODES TOWN

Minos Pension £ A charming pension on the highest spot of the Old Town, with magnificent views from the rooms and rooftop café. ⓐ 5 Omirou, Rhodes Town ⓣ 22410 31813 ⓦ www.minospension.com

TINGAKI

Tigaki Beach Hotel ££ A large complex beside the sea with air-conditioned rooms, a garden and pool. A short walk to the centre. ⓐ Beach road, Tingaki ⓣ 22420 69446 ⓦ www.tigakibeach-kos.com

Preparing to go

GETTING THERE

The cheapest way to get to Rhodes or Kos is to book a package holiday with one of the leading tour operators. Those specialising in Crete offer flight-only deals or combined flight-and-accommodation packages at prices that are hard to beat by booking direct. The flight time from London is 4–5 hours. If you're booked on a smaller island, the trip may involve a flight followed by a ferry ride. There are numerous charter airline companies offering flights to Rhodes during the summer months, although if you travel out of season, you may have to use a scheduled flight with British Airways (☎ 0870 850 9 850 ⓦ www.ba.com) or Olympic Airlines (☎ 0870 60 60 460 ⓦ www.olympicairlines.com) to Athens and a connecting flight with Olympic Airlines or the better quality Aegean Airlines (☎ +30 210 626 1000 ⓦ www.aegeanair.com) to Rhodes or Kos. You can also choose to use one of many budget airlines flying to Greece: see ⓦ www.whichbudget.com for a complete overview of connections. If you can be flexible about when you visit, you can pick up relatively inexpensive special deals. As a rule, the further in advance you buy your ticket, the cheaper it usually is – but you can also get good last-minute deals from online travel agents via the internet.

Many people are aware that air travel emits CO_2, which contributes to climate change. You may be interested in the possibility of lessening the environmental impact of your flight through the charity Climate Care, which offsets your CO_2 by funding environmental projects around the world. Visit ⓦ www.climatecare.org

TOURISM AUTHORITY

In the UK, the **Greek National Tourist Office** (ⓐ 4 Conduit Street, London W1S 2DJ ☎ 020 7495 9300 ⓔ info@gnto.co.uk ⓦ www.gnto.co.uk) can provide general information about visiting Greece, and has useful brochures and maps that you can download online or order. The official **Rhodes Town website** has a wealth of historical information and tips. Visit ⓦ www.rhodes.gr

BEFORE YOU LEAVE

It is not necessary to have inoculations to travel in Europe, but you should make sure you and your family are up to date with the basics, such as tetanus. It is a good idea to pack a small first-aid kit to carry with you containing plasters, antiseptic cream, travel sickness pills, insect repellent and/or bite-relief cream, antihistamine tablets, upset stomach remedies and painkillers. Suntan lotion and after-sun cream are more expensive in Greece than in the UK so it is worth taking some. Take your prescription medicines along as you may find it impossible to obtain the same medicines in Greece.

Although Greece is a very safe country when it comes to petty crime and has a good healthcare system, it's a good idea to purchase travel insurance before you go. Check the policy carefully regarding medical coverage, dental treatment, loss of baggage, flight cancellations, repatriation, etc., and whether activities like scuba diving, horse riding and watersports need extra coverage. Keep all medical receipts for claim purposes; if your possessions are stolen, you'll also need to file a police report. UK visitors carrying a European Health Insurance Card (EHIC) get reduced-cost and sometimes free state-provided medical treatment in Greece and most other European countries. The free card can be ordered via the Department of Health (☏ 0845 606 2030 Ⓦ www.ehic.org.uk).

ENTRY FORMALITIES

All EU and other citizens from all Western countries only need a passport to enter Greece. Visas are only required by certain nationalities; details can be found on the **Greek Foreign Ministry** website Ⓦ www.mfa.gr. All children, including newborn babies, need their own passports unless they are already included on the passport of the person they are travelling with. For the latest information on passports, contact the Identity & Passport Service (☏ 0870 521 0410 Ⓦ www.passport.gov.uk). Check the details of your travel tickets well before your departure, ensuring that the timings and dates are correct. If you plan to rent a car in Greece, be sure to have your driving licence (and that of any other driver) with you.

MONEY

Like many EU countries, Greece uses the euro. Euro (€) note denominations are 500, 200, 100, 50, 20, 10 and 5. Coins are 1 and 2 euros and 1, 2, 5, 10, 20 and 50 centimos (also called *lepta*). The best way to get euros in Greece is by using your debit card in an ATM (cash machine), which can be found in all towns, resorts and airports. Make sure you know your PIN and check with your bank to see if there are any charges for using your card abroad. Credit cards are increasingly accepted in hotels and restaurants on Rhodes and Kos, but less so in shops and supermarkets. Check the validity date and credit limit of your cards before you go. You can purchase cash euros before leaving the UK, but keep in mind that changing cash locally at a bank or exchange office will be much better value. Euro-denomination traveller's cheques, which can be purchased at UK exchange offices and banks, are a safe way to carry money as you'll be refunded if the cheques are lost or stolen, but they're used less and less in Europe and can be a hassle to change. If you are going to Turkey, you can easily change euros or sterling into Turkish lira on arrival.

CLIMATE

Rhodians enjoy a typical Mediterranean climate: hot, dry summers and cool, wet winters. From May to September you will hardly see a day of rain. July and August are rather hot – it is best to stay out of the sun from 11.00–15.00. The climate in Kos is good from May to November, but from September to April it can get wet and windy. The best dress rule to follow is to wear layers so that if you get too hot, you only need to remove a shirt or sweater. A light jacket or cardigan is a must for early evenings at the beginning and end of the season. Average daytime temperatures on the islands are: April 16°C (61°F); May 20°C (68°F); June 26°C (78°F); July 27°C (81°F); August 27°C (81°F); September 25°C (77°F); October 20°C (68°F).

BAGGAGE ALLOWANCE

Baggage allowances vary according to the airline, destination and the class of travel, but 20 kg (44 lb) per person is the norm for luggage that is carried in the hold; check your ticket to see if the weight limit is mentioned there. Large items – surfboards, golf-clubs, collapsible wheelchairs and pushchairs – are usually charged as extras, and it is a good idea to let the airline know in advance if you want to bring these. You are allowed only one item of hand baggage measuring 55 by 40 by 20 cm (22 by 16 by 8 in) plus any airport purchases, umbrella, handbag, coat, camera, etc. Note that security measures at both UK and Greek airports prohibit you from taking any sharp objects or any liquids and gels in your hand baggage, except liquids necessary for the flight and packed in containers no larger than 100 ml (3½ oz) inside a resealable plastic bag. Read more about the security rules on your departure airport website.

⬥ *Travel by hydrofoil from Rhodes or Kos to Bodrum or Marmaris in Turkey*

During your stay

AIRPORTS

The airports on Rhodes and Kos are small and often crowded. Both airports are served by good roads. Taxis are readily available at both airports, and many rental car agencies have offices at the airports. Note that it's often cheaper to arrange car hire in advance, and that in high season cars can be difficult to come by without advance booking. You can also get to Rhodes town by the frequent airport bus, and passengers on Olympic Airways can use the Olympic bus to get to Kos Town.

Car hire

Drivers need to be over 21 (25 in some cases) and have a valid driving licence. Car hire is available at all resorts and costs €30–60 per day for a small car, depending on season and length of rental. Local rental companies in the beach resorts often have lower prices than the international companies in the main towns. Most rental cars are new and zippy small cars, and air-conditioning is quite common. Open-top 4WDs are popular too but much pricier. Insurance is included in your car rental, but is sometimes not valid if you use non-asphalted roads, and check that it includes damage to the wheels, tyres and roof.

COMMUNICATIONS

The Greek national phone company, **OTE**, has public phones in all towns, villages and resorts which accept OTE phone cards and have English-language instructions. Some resorts have private coin-operated phone booths but these are usually very bad value. You can also make calls from many kiosks or from a kafenion in smaller villages; they have a metering system and you will be told how much your call costs at the end. Using a €5 prepaid calling card (available at any kiosk) is the cheapest way to phone abroad. These can be used from any OTE public phone or hotel phone.

Many tourists bring their mobile phones along and use roaming to phone home. Check the charges carefully as this can be a very expensive way to phone home. If you're planning to phone often and want to be reached as well, consider buying a local Cosmote or Vodafone SIM card (available from many kiosks and mobile phone shops for a few euros) so you have a local number incurring lower costs.

Post offices

Most post offices are open 08.00–14.30 Mon–Fri, the main ones in Rhodes and Kos Towns until 19.30 and Sat. During the tourist season there are also mobile post offices, big yellow caravans, which appear in several tourist areas. They are often open at weekends. Post boxes are bright yellow with a blue logo on; at major post offices you will find two slots; *esoterik* for local mail and *exoterik* for overseas. Outside the main towns they are not always emptied every day. Postcards can take up to

TELEPHONING TO AND IN GREECE

All telephone numbers in Greece, whether landline or mobile phones, consist of 10 digits, and there are no additional city codes. To make a call within Greece, simply dial these ten digits. To call to Greece from abroad or from your mobile phone while in the country, dial the international access code, usually 00, followed by Greece's country code +30 and the ten-digit local number.

TELEPHONING ABROAD

To call abroad from Greece, dial 00 followed by the country code followed by the city code (minus the initial 0) and the subscriber's number.

44 for the UK
353 for Ireland
1 for the US and Canada
61 for Australia
64 for New Zealand
27 for South Africa

two weeks to get to Britain, letters three or four days; if you want your postcards to arrive back home before you do then put them in an envelope. Sending a postcard or letter abroad costs €0.62.

CUSTOMS

Greeks are usually very friendly to strangers, and you are bound to experience traditional hospitality in one way or another during your stay. Greeks rarely begin their evening meal earlier than 21.00, and usually take the whole family along, babies too. Children are generally allowed to wander around restaurants at will, even late at night.

DRESS CODES

If you are visiting churches or monasteries you will not be allowed in wearing shorts or beach clothes; it is best to wear long trousers or a skirt and take a shirt or wrap to cover your shoulders. Some churches provide clothing for visitors to dress up in. Topless sunbathing is officially forbidden but still common in some beach resorts; judge the situation before stripping and causing upset.

ELECTRICITY

Rhodes and Kos have 220 V/50 hertz electrical outlets. You will need an adaptor plug for any electrical equipment you bring with you and these can be purchased at the local supermarkets or in the UK before you depart. At times in high season there may be power-cuts lasting at most two hours, but usually much less. It is important to realise that electricity is expensive in Greece, so be considerate and do not leave lights and air conditioning on in your room when you go out.

GETTING AROUND
Driving conditions
Remember that in Greece you drive on the right. Always carry your driving licence, passport and any other relevant documents with you when driving, and ask for a map when renting the car. The road quality on Rhodes and Kos is generally quite good, with only smaller roads and

EMERGENCIES
ambulance, **police** and **fire brigade** 112
tourist police in Rhodes Town (ⓣ 22410 27423) and
Kos Town (ⓣ 22420 26666)
hospitals of Rhodes Town (ⓣ 22410 80000) and Kos Town
(ⓣ 22420 22300)

unsurfaced tracks requiring you to slow down to protect your wheel rims.
You may experience traffic jams when leaving or entering Rhodes. Beyond
the main resorts, Rhodes' roads are mostly deserted. Kos has only one
main road running the length of the island. On major roads, what would
appear to be the hard shoulder is used to allow faster traffic to pass. In
high season beware slow drivers, holidaymakers on quad motorbikes,
farmers watering their olives and traffic jams. Parking in Rhodes Town can
be a problem, and it's wise to stay out of the centre area and find a spot in
the parking areas along the harbourfront – the ones a little further from
the centre are free. Blue lines on the street indicate paid parking, yellow
lines official services only, white lines are free parking.

If you are stopped by the police for a motoring offence you are
expected to pay your fine on the spot (make sure you get a receipt if you
do). If you do not pay, the police will remove the licence plates from your
car, which you will then have to reclaim from the police station on
payment of the fine. Contact your hire company if this happens.

Public transport
Buses are cheap and quite good on Rhodes and Kos. All buses are air-
conditioned coaches and usually run on time. In cities, printed
timetables can be found at the tourist offices and at the bus station,
where you can also buy tickets in advance. When getting on in villages
and resorts you usually pay the conductor after getting seated. In
Rhodes, all buses leave from the two adjacent bus stations near
Mandraki harbour. In Kos town, buses leave from the stops on Kleopatras
street, just south of the town centre.

Taxis

Taxis can be found at arrival points, major hotels and driving around the larger resorts. They're comparatively inexpensive to use, and prices for longer distances are usually fixed. There's a surcharge after midnight. Any hotel or restaurant will call a taxi for you on request.

HEALTH, SAFETY & CRIME

Healthcare

There are a number of private medical clinics offering a 24-hour service with English-speaking doctors. Details are available at local pharmacies. *Pharmakia* (pharmacies) often have English-speaking staff and are very helpful for minor complaints and illnesses. Generally both over-the-counter and prescription drugs purchased at pharmacies will be cheaper than in England. However, some, such as antibiotics, can be expensive. You should bring your EHIC with you – the old E111 form – to receive reduced-cost or free medical treatment (see page 115).

Water

Tap water is safe enough, but bottled water is widely available, cheap and tastes much better.

Safety & crime

Compared with most western European countries, Greece is a very safe place, with hardly any petty or violent crime. A forgotten camera or wallet will most likely still be on the restaurant table when you return for it, and public drunkenness or violence is quite rare. Still, avoid temptation by leaving all valuables and documents in the hotel safe and carrying only what you need. Watch out for bag snatchers in busy resorts and towns, and leave your car empty when you park it. The police keep a low profile but invariably turn up when needed at motor accidents and crime scenes, and to deal with illegally parked cars. Parking in the narrow streets of towns and villages can be a problem. The police may show tolerance towards local inhabitants over parking, but are less inclined to treat hire cars with the same degree of leniency. There are also tourist police, who speak several languages and are trained to help with problems faced by tourists.

MEDIA

It's easy to stay in touch with home, as even the smaller resorts sell English newspapers, usually only a day or two out of date. Locally produced newspapers in English can be a useful source of information about local events. Most hotels with televisions and English bars have satellite TV for a dose of sports and news. The online English edition of Greece's *Kathimerini* newspaper is a good source of national news (ⓦ www.ekathimerini.com). There's also a section detailing festivals around Greece.

OPENING HOURS

Shops traditionally open from 08.00–14.30 Mon & Wed, 08.00–14.00 & 17.00–20.00 Tues, Thur, Fri and 08.00–13.00 Sat. Tourist resorts are a case apart and most shops open all day, usually from early morning until 23.00. Sunday is a general closing day, but shops serving tourism mostly remain open.

Banks are open 08.00–14.00 Mon–Thur and 08.00–13.30 Fri. A few branches in Rhodes Town, Kos Town and Lindos are also open from 09.00–13.00 Sat.

Restaurants are generally often open 09.00–23.00. Breakfast ends around 10.00, lunch is usually between 13.30–15.30 and dinner starts late for Greeks – 20.00 is on the early side.

Churches are almost always open for visiting, but in villages you often have to find the lady in black who looks after the key.

RELIGION

Greece is dominated by the Greek Orthodox Church with a faith that has strong historical roots in the local community. Saints' days and name days are very important days to celebrate. Weddings, baptisms and funerals are serious and lengthy occasions. Be respectful and cover up before you enter a church or chapel.

TIME DIFFERENCES

Greece is in the Eastern European Time zone (EET). During Eastern European Summertime, it is BST+2 and during Eastern European Standard Time it is GMT+3. Greece is CST-8, EST-7 and PST-10.

TIPPING

In restaurants a service or cover charge is often included in your bill. However, if the service warrants it you can leave a small tip to the waiters or bar staff; 5–10 per cent is about right. Taxi drivers don't expect tips but if you are happy with the service, give a tip. If you are shown around a church by the 'keyholder' or priest, a tip is also welcome, but this should always be left in the donations box rather than offered directly to the guide.

TOILETS

Public toilets are found in bus stations and main squares. Smarter facilities are found in bars, but you should buy a drink or ask nicely if you want to use them. Toilets are generally very clean, but you must observe the practice throughout Greece and not flush away used toilet paper. Do as the Greeks do and put it in a bin (provided in each cubicle) next to the toilet. Remember this, or you risk blocking the pipes!

TRAVELLERS WITH DISABILITIES

Greece is slowly catching up with the rest of the EU when it comes to facilities for the disabled, with Rhodes a step ahead of Kos. Many ramps have now been built onto beaches and in hotel and restaurant entrances, and some of the local buses have disabled access, but this is normally restricted to people on foot, not in wheelchairs. You may experience some difficulty while visiting archaeological sites, so it is best to travel with assistance. Rhodes' Old Town has cobblestones and hills that can be tiring for those who are less able; Kos town is flat and easier to get around. Some hotels in Kos have facilities for disabled people, but there are very few taxis or even buses that can cope with a motorised wheelchair.

ACKNOWLEDGEMENTS

The publishers would like to thank the following individuals and organisations for providing their photographs for this book, to whom the copyright belongs:

Age Fotostock/Superstock page 19; Kath Freer/Spanish Tourist Office page 106; Horvat/Wikimedia Commons page 86; Pictures Colour Library pages 75; Jozsef Szasz-Fabian/BigStockPhoto.com page 10–11; Jeroen van Marle pages 43, 50, 69, 71, 93, 99, 111, 117; Steve Vidler/SuperStock page 105; World Pictures/Photoshot pages 22, 25, 69; all the rest Thomas Cook Tour Operations Limited

Project editor: Alison Coupe
Layout: Donna Pedley
Proofreader: Amanda Jones
Indexer: Marie Lorimer

Send your thoughts to
books@thomascook.com

- Found a beach bar, peaceful stretch of sand or must-see sight that we don't feature?

- Like to tip us off about any information that needs a little updating?

- Want to tell us what you love about this handy, little guidebook and more importantly how we can make it even handier?

Then here's your chance to tell all! Send us ideas, discoveries and recommendations today and then look out for your valuable input in the next edition of this title.

Send an email to the above address or write to:
HotSpots Series Editor, Thomas Cook Publishing, PO Box 227, Unit 9, Coningsby Road, Peterborough PE3 8SB, UK.